ALMOST HOME

ALMOST HOME

By Maggie and David Cavagnaro

As told by David

Illustrated by the Authors

IMAGES OF AMERICA SERIES

AMERICAN WEST PUBLISHING COMPANY
PALO ALTO, CALIFORNIA

To Pippin and all children,
who hold the potential for a viable future

ACKNOWLEDGMENTS

In a sense, everyone we have known—and some people we have never met whose influence has reached us nevertheless—has helped us to chart a course in life that led to the creation of this book. We would like to express our particular gratitude, however, to those friends who have helped us with the project itself: All those at Audubon Canyon Ranch who have made our experiences there possible; the students who have taught us much about the learning process; the research associates, whose ceaseless work, enthusiasm, and good humor have helped nurture an idea toward the future; Pat Kollings and George Pfeiffer of American West, who have stood beside us with their talents and patience through the birth of three books; Milton Cavagnaro, who has stood beside us through just about everything, and all the rest of our family, whose understanding has given us strength; Steve Kimball and all other members of our spiritual family; and Hansel and Otto Hagel, who in the free sharing of their unity and way of life gave us the courage to begin this journey together.

Library of Congress Cataloging in Publication Data

Cavagnaro, David.   Almost home.

  (Images of America series)
  1. Country life—California—Pictorial works. 2. Photography, Artistic.
3. Cavagnaro, David. 4. Cavagnaro, Maggie, 1943–
I. Cavagnaro, Maggie, 1943–   ill.   II. Title.

S521.5.C2C38   979.4'62   74-83337
ISBN 0-910118-58-2
ISBN 0-910118-59-0 deluxe

FIRST EDITION

Contents

Beginning a Life

Because of our love for the natural world and our work with children, Maggie and I had become dissatisfied with the pace and values of urban living. Slowly the need for change swelled within us, much as the embryo of a seed pushes against its walls once it has received the touch of water. At last we decided that we must search for a new life in a place where we might know the natural world in all its moods and learn from it the intricate balance that sustains all living things, where we might use our hands and our minds in creative ways, where we might grow our own food and raise our family in a spirit of joy and discovery, where we might understand from direct experience the significance of life and death, the satisfaction of hard work and accomplishment, and the fulfillment of sharing with others whatever we might learn. Somehow, we agreed, we must find a place called "home." This search we have begun together, even though we know that it may require a lifetime.

In the spring we moved to Audubon Canyon Ranch,
a wildlife sanctuary near the shore of the Pacific. From
the century-old farmhouse we could hear sea gulls
calling and the distant surf crashing.

It was in a sense an emergence. Like the flowers of meadow and forest, we were reaching for the sun and the earth, striving for a new beginning. Within a week of our arrival Pippin was born. Isolated as we had been from the basic processes of life, nothing in our past had prepared us for the magnificent experience of the birth of our son.

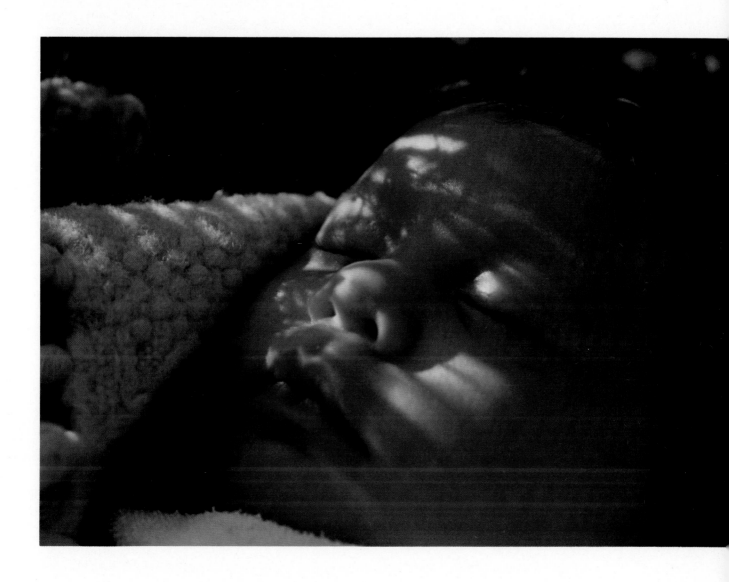

With Pippin slung in a swath of cloth, together as a family
we began to explore our surroundings. As the cooling fog
of summer rolled in against the land, the mysteries of forest,
grassland, marsh, and lagoon gradually unfolded before us.

October rains ended the long spell of California summer. A reawakening gripped the land. The canyon stream began to flow with stronger voice; steelhead returned to the sea; frogs began their courtship chorus, and stately bucks in rut paraded through the ranch yard after does. While the pulse thus quickened for some, the chill of autumn nights brought dormancy to trees and shrubs in a final flurry of color.

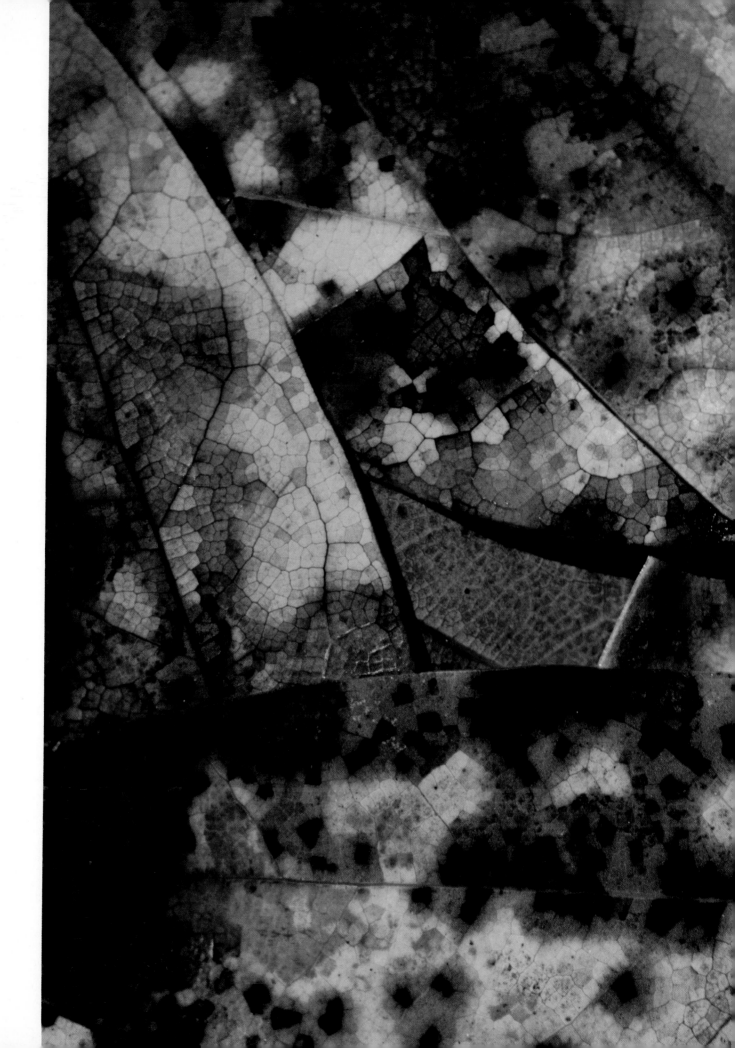

Winter revealed the power of the Pacific Ocean. Storm after storm ripped in against the coast. Trees fell and the swollen stream tore at its canyon walls.

These turbulent days and the calm moments in between were the best times to be out on the land absorbing events with all our senses. We were gradually becoming familiar with the rhythms of nature and learning to live in harmony with them. A way of life had begun to take possession of us. This was not so much accident as choice.

I

BIRTH

Maggie and I drove up the narrow dirt road to our cabin. The sun had just cleared the ridge across the valley, and steam was beginning to rise from frost-covered stems on the rose fence beyond the kitchen window. Inside, we stoked the wood stove and set some breakfast on to simmer.

Winter still gripped the land. We had been out in the valley since dawn, poking through the crystalline night mantle, searching the frosted grass with mind and camera for what inspiration and understanding we could find there. It was one of many such walks we had taken that year. As we worked on the last parts of our book *This Living Earth*, each contact with the complex and beautiful story of the grassland seemed to reinforce our bond with the natural world.

The smell of hot coffee, toast, and omelette filled the kitchen. As we ate by the crackling Franklin, we began to talk of our morning walks in the meadows, of our life together, and the direction our experiences seemed to be leading us. We agreed that we were ready for a change.

Our tiny rented cabin in the San Geronimo Valley had been adequate for three years. It was compact and cozy, allowed us proximity both to the schools in the suburbs where we worked as free-lance biology teachers and to the wild places we had been exploring while we completed our book. Our surroundings were somewhat rural, and we had enough yard for a modest vegetable garden. Still, our first child was on the way, and our own needs had grown so that we knew we would soon want a larger house.

The desire for an extra room or two, however, was only a small part of the thirst for change that welled up within us. We were dissatisfied, tired of driving all over the countryside from job to job, tired of bucking the traffic and fighting the blighted urban views. We had been working for several years with teachers and with classes of schoolchildren, but the time in these programs was never long enough. We yearned for a way to share the thrill of exploration and discovery in the outdoors in a deeper, more sustained way.

The need for change reached even deeper within us than this. When we were first married, Maggie and I, like most everyone else, lived in town and held routine, full-time jobs. On weekends and holidays we broke loose from our daily affairs and drove off in search of solitude in some wild place. In those days we went most often to the distant Sierra Nevada, where we hiked and backpacked among the peaks and alpine meadows.

Our move out of town and the switch to a free-lance means of livelihood allowed us more frequent contact with the natural world. As we explored the landscapes closer to home, we began to under-stand more clearly that our roots as a species lay somewhere among the natural laws that give order to the rivers, the mountains, the fields, and the myriad creatures that inhabit them. The more we experienced the laws of nature at work around us and the more sensitive we became to their sig-nificance, the more dissatisfied we had grown with the consumption-oriented, helter-skelter way of life to which we were exposed day after day.

And then we also had to ask ourselves what kind of life we wanted to provide for our child. We had passed the formative years long ago, and we had so far convinced ourselves that we were adaptable to almost any set of conditions. But our work with children had made certain in our minds that the early years of childhood are im-portant beyond compare. There is no turning back entirely the first chapters of one's life.

We wondered if we wanted to raise our child on television and a dozen store-bought presents each Christmas. We asked ourselves if we wanted our child to spend an hour or more every day in an automobile, listening to noise and breathing fumes, to eat a diet of processed foods and be processed himself by a culture dominated by com-petition and consumption. We wondered what effect we would have upon our child as parents if we were isolated from the values and surround-ings that meant most to us.

If we were to accept as real and valid the values we had gradually developed over the years from our experience with young people and our contact with nature, then it seemed only right that we begin to explore these values not merely as a weekend pastime, not merely as a schoolbook lesson to be fed now and then to our child and to

the children of others, but instead to employ them as a way of life.

The next weeks were a time of searching. We explored our feelings, talked about politics and schools, discussed other parts of the world we had visited in the past, studied maps, and thought about buying land. But the more we analyzed our alternatives, the more we understood that we were ready to make a change not so much of place as of living itself. After all, this region had always been our home. We had grown up here. We loved the land and knew something of the plants and animals that lived on it. Our friends, our family, and everything we could call familiar, were here.

We had both traveled enough to know that there is no escape from corrupt government, over-population, environmental degradation, and the tensions of living in the twentieth century. These are problems we share with all men. What, then, would we gain by running away? Why should we leave our home and our heritage when we had just begun to learn what these things really were and what we ourselves could make of them?

We decided that we must look for a place in our immediate neighborhood, surrounded by wild-ness, where we might live, teach, and raise our child in harmony with the principles of the nat-ural world; where we might grow most of our own food and learn again the skills of basic living; yet where we would be close enough to urban American culture that we might both partake of its strengths and return to it something of what we might gain from our own experience.

A short distance north and a little west of San Francisco lies the vast expanse of Point Reyes National Seashore. Beyond the dark forested slopes of Inverness Ridge, the land pitches grad-ually toward the sea. Point Reyes itself juts straight into the incessant Pacific winds. Battered by storms in winter and fog winds in summer, the grassy moors and jagged cliffs of the peninsula are seldom quiet. Cries of gulls, the bark of sea lions, and the constant crash of surf form the main vocabulary of this coastal wilderness. Above the background conversation rise a thousand other voices, and on calm spring days, when the wave calls are softened, bees hum in brilliant meadows.

Point Reyes Peninsula is separated from the bulk of central California by the San Andreas Fault, powerful destroyer of cities and sculptor of the land. The gradual, and sometimes not so gradual, slippage of the peninsula northward along the fault has etched into the landscape a long, straight valley, which to the north is submerged beneath Tomales Bay and to the south dips again beneath Bolinas Lagoon. These two

bodies of water are among the last wild lagoons and estuaries left on the western shore of the United States.

Protected from westerly winds by Inverness Ridge and Bolinas Mesa and from pounding surf by the curving sandspit of Stinson Beach, the rich mud flats and salt marshes of Bolinas Lagoon are refuge and feeding ground for tens of thousands of seabirds. In the winter, when the migrants are in, the lagoon may be nearly covered from side to side with waterfowl and shorebirds, and in the spring great blue herons and great egrets arrive to nest at Audubon Canyon Ranch.

The Ranch is a wildlife sanctuary established in 1961 to protect the herons and egrets that return each year to nest in the redwoods of one steep, wooded canyon on the watershed of the lagoon. Since then the Ranch has helped to ensure the preservation of the lagoon and has grown to include three other adjacent canyons, two nearby groves where monarch butterflies overwinter, and the extensive Audubon Cypress Grove Refuge on Tomales Bay.

Since Maggie and I had been teaching part time at the Ranch rookery, it was by a happy chance of timing that we were present when the directors of the Ranch needed further help in developing an education program. They had decided to establish one of the canyons of the sanctuary as an outdoor education center and asked us to help carry out this endeavor while in residence there.

Together we went to take a look at the setting. The canyon seemed deeper and longer than the one we knew from our teaching experience. Toward the bottom of the ridge, the dark, forested slopes parted widely, the stream emerged through groves of giant alders, and in the flat bottomland stood a white, century-old farmhouse, echoing still the sentiments and craftsmanship of its builder, a Bostonian sea captain who had settled here beside the Pacific. In the ranch yard we found a few ancient apple trees, a ranch hand's shanty, and a lichen-covered longhouse, built of virgin redwood and still leaning from the San Francisco earthquake of 1906. Below the buildings stretched a magnificent expanse of marsh, and beyond that lay the lagoon itself.

The canyon was more than we had expected. It was a world in one sense apart yet connected in myriad ways to the rest of the natural world that webs the earth. This place would offer us solitude but not isolation. That we might live in a place so beautiful, so primeval, so close to our past as well as our present, exceeded even our dreams of a place we could call home.

After our visit it was mutually agreed that we would join the sanctuary as resident biologists, move to the Ranch, and begin work on the development of an outdoor education program.

By then winter was yielding to warmer days. Spring planting time was upon us, our goat Sunflower was pregnant, and our own child was due any moment. We raced against time, building a goat house and pen, preparing a large garden plot, and fencing it against the deer. The very first thing we moved to the canyon was our compost pile! Next came Sunflower and Snowballs, the beginning of our goat herds.

On moving day itself we had a large gathering of family and friends. Together we succeeded in moving nearly everything from our little cabin to the old ranch house, and when the work was done, we shared in the joy and satisfaction of a big feast. A dozen or more deer hovered around the perimeter of the ranch yard, and that night, as we sat quietly amid the clutter of boxes and furniture, a grey fox came up to the dining-room window and peered in to survey the new tenants.

Five days after we moved to Audubon Canyon Ranch, our son was born. There is nothing in the natural world more beautiful or more amazing than the arrival of new life. As a child I had watched more times than I can remember tiny caterpillars hatching from delicate eggs, and watched again as they emerged from dormancy, transformed from sedentary leaf-munchers into fragile creatures of the air. When we lived in town, I saw newborn kittens spread out neatly on the bed nursing while our dog, Bo, hovered over them with wrinkled-brow paternal concern. But nothing in my past prepared me for the magnificent experience of watching the birth of our son.

From the beginning of Maggie's pregnancy, we both had wanted our child to be born by natural childbirth. We signed up with an excellent team of doctors who treat prenatal care and delivery as a simple, joyous affair rather than a strictly medical process. Even with their guidance, however, we quickly learned how far our cultural heritage had removed us from what would otherwise be the most beautiful, natural event in our lives.

As we attended regular childbirth classes, we found ourselves surrounded by people who were almost totally ignorant about pregnancy and birth. We could read from the faces in the room that misinformation had passed from one generation to the next, and fears bred from long cultural neglect and avoidance of basic biological facts were not easily dispelled. Even Maggie and I, with our backgrounds in biology and our understanding of anatomy, discovered many gaps in our knowledge. We were learning for the first time, as we would again and again in our new life at the Ranch, how deep the chasm had grown between us and the simple biological processes that our species has dealt with intimately for all but the last moments of its long evolution.

Maggie felt the first signs of labor early on the morning of April 30. After dressing amid a heap of partially unpacked boxes, we walked out into the cool air of dawn. A few stars still penetrated the half-light, and bats were just returning to their roosts in the longhouse attic. Maggie was relaxed and not at all in a hurry. Near the top of the winding mountain road that leads to San Francisco, she asked to stop for a stretch and a look at the sunrise. Before I knew what was happening, she was off down the hillside in search of wild flowers! For Maggie, at least, the break with the past had been partially bridged, and her confidence was reassuring.

Once she was in the hospital, labor came slowly, building, tapering off, building again. Finally, shortly after noon, the pace quickened, and we joined a nurse in the delivery room. Maggie took the contractions in stride, while I mopped her forehead and chanted the rhythms of relaxation. The doctor was late, arriving just barely in time to assist as the child began to emerge. In what seemed like another instant, he was out screaming in the foreign air, and then he was in Maggie's arms dozing and nuzzling peacefully, listening again to the heartbeat from which he had momentarily been separated. Six-and-a-half pounds. A son.

Nothing, neither our inexperience nor the medicinal atmosphere of the delivery room, could dampen the spirit of that moment. The feelings that overwhelmed us were too much a part of our ancient lineage to be held back by a short span of cultural tampering. Together we had crossed the chasm.

Of all the forms of life that have evolved on earth, man alone seems to sense the weight of time. Decades, centuries, millennia, and eons are abstractions we ourselves have created as arbitrary guideposts marking pathways into the past, and yet we are certain that the passage of time that they represent has been real. We alone know this, for no other creature is aware, beyond the consciousness of its own life experiences and the unconscious time record in its genetic code, that the relentless march of time has left its marks along the way.

The birth of our son reached toward our ancestors and from them clear back to the dim origins of man. His birth contained also the history of the reptiles from which mammals evolved, of the ancient amphibians that gave rise to reptiles long before, of the primeval ooze in some warm, shallow sea where all life had its beginning, even of the birth of our solar system, and of countless other celestial beginnings long ago obscured by the onward rush of time.

Though this unique awareness of the past is part of our potential, we are seldom conscious of it. We live mostly in the present because, like other creatures, we must in order to survive. The birth of our son broke through this veneer of immediacy that encases us. His arrival was far more than an event of the present, more even than a symbol of new life. It was a continuation.

For many months after his arrival in the family, he had no name. We tried the usual approaches—consulting family and friends, and browsing through numerous books designed to assist in the customary process. For more than a year he was known by a dozen different names, Paolo, Devon, Joaquin, Jamile, and Wort among them, according to each person's particular preference. But at last, through some mysterious alchemy that has yet to be understood, our son became known to us and to all as Pippin.

Sunflower's first offspring arrived less than a week after Pippin was born. By calculation, Maggie had anticipated their arrival, but it was only through the peculiar psychic tuning of motherhood that she knew to awake out of a sound sleep at two o'clock in the morning so that she might check on Sunflower. I decided that I had better get dressed, too, so that I could assist with the inevitable, and I was just lacing my boots when Maggie ran back into the house with a bundle in her arms. Wrapped in a towel was a tiny heap of wet fur with long, drooping ears and as beautiful a face as I had ever seen. We wrapped the little goat snugly in a box. Since Pippin was only four days old, the compulsion of motherhood would not allow Maggie to leave him in the house, so, she wrapped him up and placed him, too, in a box. With Pippin under one arm and an empty box under the other, I accompanied Maggie back to the pen.

Sunflower was getting ready to deliver the afterbirth. We knew there had to be another baby around somewhere, for she had been big enough across the middle to produce a small elephant. We had looked high and low in every corner of Sunflower's house and pen, and had nearly given up the search when we heard a faint bleat from beneath the house. Curled up in a far recess that was completely dry and protected from the cold wind, we found Sunflower's firstborn, thoroughly cleaned by its mother, its fur dry and warm.

Not to feel completely unneeded, we dragged the little kid out, placed it in the empty box, and took it with us to the ranch house. Sunflower allowed our participation without protest. Once again in the bedroom, we lined the three boxes up by the heater, the two kid goats and Pippin, and went back to sleep.

At the first light of morning, we took the frisky little goats back to the pen, and they immediately went for a long drink of warm milk. We gave them names—Tinga and Sienna—as our final stamp of authority over the small herd, but we had discovered that in spite of the many centuries goats have spent with man, the veneer of domestication is thin. Sunflower came happily to us at feeding time, and later, as the kids were weaned, she jumped readily onto the milk stand, but otherwise she and her instincts were fully in charge.

Thus began our life at Audubon Canyon Ranch. Within a span of nine days we had assumed responsibility for a new member of our own family, a goat herd double its former number, a garden potentially four times the size of the one we had before, one of the area's most significant historical buildings, and an embryonic plan for an outdoor education program.

My father, Milton, and a college student named Steve came to live and work with us for the summer in order to prepare the canyon for teaching. Steve built a catwalk so that the freshwater marsh could be used as a study area with maximum convenience and minimum damage to fragile plant life. Ponds were dug so that we would have open areas of water in which to observe aquatic life. The longhouse was outfitted with work benches, shelving, shop space, and our accumulated collections of tools and specimens. We had grounds to maintain, trails to build, teaching programs to design for the autumn months ahead, and the incessant chain of diapers to attend to. We seldom left the ranch yard and the work of the day.

In time, however, we began to explore our surroundings, starting with the stream and marsh nearby, and gradually working farther into the rugged canyon, across the grassy bluffs, and along the shore of the lagoon. During the storms and frosts of winter, the dripping fogs of summer, and the crystalline mornings of spring and fall when the world seemed to surpass every utopian dream, we were out feeling, watching, learning.

During our earliest explorations of the canyon, Pippin came along with us in the backpack, taking in with his senses and recording with his brain every possible aspect of his new environment. Soon he was crawling about the ranch yard, feeling, probing, pulling, testing. As he became adept with language, he was able to tell us with certainty the name of the bird behind almost every call. He could identify principal trees and flowers, and was soon able to explain in simple terms the processes he had seen at work long before speech had given voice to his observations. Before the age of three Pippin was in the lead on the trail, showing us and the students what he had discovered about the world we share.

This is the natural apprenticeship of childhood. Children of the native tribes that once inhabited this coast had learned many of the same things in much the same sequence for thousands of years before, part of the constantly repeated and gradually refined growth pattern inherent in our species.

We have now lived at the Ranch for three years. In that time we have grown most of our food and learned some of the skills necessitated by a basic life-style. We have also tried a number of experimental teaching programs; some have been rejected, and some have remained as successful ventures in the learning process. Though our life together has been simplified, the need to earn a livelihood has remained, and for this we have depended upon our teaching, art, writing, and photography. We have therefore had to face the problem of balancing creative work against the time-consuming task of providing for our own sustenance, and we have had to learn also to balance our need for solitude against our need to be with other people.

In some ways we are isolated by the pristine setting of the Ranch from the mainstream of American life. Yet in other ways we are not, for as teachers we communicate mostly with those who are far more enmeshed in contemporary society than we are. We are what might be called "partial dropouts," but we have made temporary peace with the human world that rages about us by listening intently to the sounds of its growth pains and speaking back to it, through our teaching, our creative work, and our association with other people, of the things we have learned in our own experience.

This book is only a preliminary report about what must inevitably be a lifetime endeavor. So many problems as well as satisfactions, however, have arisen early in our search that we feel compelled to share them.

We have weathered many times together, both joyous and difficult, but whatever the outcome of a given experience, we have grown closer to the earth and to each other. During these three years one of our deepest desires has been realized: to live, work, and raise our child so close to the natural world that we could feel its constant presence and begin to respond directly to its laws. No former period in Maggie's life or in mine has been so rich, no place on the earth so pervasively beautiful. Yet it was not the time, nor even the place, that was particularly special. No, we experienced what we have experienced almost entirely because we had decided to.

The rookery of great blue herons and great egrets is the central attraction that draws thousands of visitors to Audubon Canyon Ranch each spring. Either alone or with students we have climbed many times to the overlook from which nearly every nest is clearly visible. We never tire of the primeval spectacle of these birds engaged in the timeless act of survival.

Arriving singly or in groups over a period of weeks, about a hundred herons assemble in the rookery redwoods by the end of February. In the same random fashion the egrets come during March, finally numbering about a hundred seventy. We sit spellbound as the male and female egrets, each spreading a snow-white spray of nuptial plumes, bob and dance in ritual display. Their courtship is as graceful and magnificent as anything that has evolved in the world of birds, and yet when they fly toward the lagoon, their veneer of feathers somehow cannot completely camouflage their reptilian ancestry.

The ancient past seems even more immediate when the great blue herons lift from their crude stick nests and glide across the canyon redwoods for a meal along the tidal channels of the lagoon. Their serpentine necks outstretched, their guttural cries rising above the primitive background clamor of the rookery, the herons seem, in spite of their delicate plumage and grace, to be scarcely removed from the pterodactyls that long ago preceded them.

The watershed of Bolinas Lagoon is a diverse landscape containing several communities of living things. High on the ridge, above the usual level of summer fog, the rocky slopes are covered with stunted, drought-resistant and fire-tolerant shrubs of the chaparral. Below, the cool canyons are forested with Douglas firs, redwoods, California bay laurel, oaks, and buckeyes. In more open places bigleaf maples, alders, and willows border the streams. In the bottomlands there are ponds and marshes, while the bluffs overlooking the lagoon are clothed mostly in coastal shrub and grassland species. Each of the four canyons of the Ranch contains all of these communities; consequently the birdlife is rich and varied.

Of all the nesting birds, however, none has given us as much pleasure as the swallows. We have come to anticipate their arrival each spring as a great event worthy of rejoicing. Spring comes to California in waves, subtle at first, then building until the wild flowers splash a crescendo of color across the hills and valleys. Here one almost needs a

single event to give substance to the coming of spring. The arrival of the swallows has come to have this meaning for us.

The barn swallows appear first, filling the air with their staccato calls, darting in and out of attics and porches in search of nesting sites, scanning low over the grass for insects, or soaring high over the canyon. Close behind them come the violet-green and tree swallows, announcing their presence by brilliant white breasts and metallic colors rather than by voice.

Last come the cliff swallows. These gregarious birds spend the winter in Argentina. At the beginning of February, by means of some peculiar response known only within the unspoken chemistry of their genes, they turn northward and begin their incredible journey. Almost exactly a month and six thousand miles later, those that survive the hardships of migration begin arriving at the Ranch, until nearly seventy birds are soaring and circling over the ranch house. Each spring we are there watching, Maggie, Pippin, Bo, and I, and sometimes a few friends, faces turned skyward until our necks hurt, one small band welcoming their safe return just as people the world over, century upon century, have assisted the rising of the sun.

With salty mud gathered from the lagoon shore,

the cliff swallows build their gourd nests under the ranch house eaves, while barn swallows settle in various attic, porch, and woodshed niches. During our first spring, however, we could not immediately locate the nesting site of the violet-green swallow pair that frequented the canyon. A titmouse family finally solved the puzzle for us.

In one of the gnarled limbs of an apple tree in the ranch yard, we found that the titmice had constructed a nest in a hollow accessible only through one small knothole. As their young grew in size, the parent birds worked constantly bringing caterpillars and other insects from an enormous old oak several hundred yards away beyond the garden. When the young were ready to leave the nest, we were all on hand to watch the exodus. Much to our surprise, the swallows moved into the hollow the very next day. We watched the site carefully the next spring and discovered that the swallows managed to claim the apple limb first.

Of the four species, nearly ninety adult swallows occupy the canyon each year. As we watched their activity, we wondered about the food supply necessary to support this number, especially as they began feeding young. Our attention was drawn to the marsh, for this rank, boggy place seemed to be a prime source for the incredible volume of insects consumed by the adults and brought to the nests each day.

The marsh, like the rookery, is a place from another time, out of context, separated from the present by the aura of history that seeps up from soggy earth and decaying roots. The marsh in front of the ranch house is young, created only recently by a simple change in the nearby road. Even in terms of evolutionary time, many of the plants that occupy it are recent arrivals in the world. Yet they grow side by side with horsetails and ferns, and they seem to yield to the authority of these ancient plants. Marshes are in a way the last stronghold for these primitive refugees of the plant kingdom, and wherever marshes spring up on the face of the land, it is as though the ferns and horsetails have

wrested a piece of the earth as their own, dragging it back to a previous age and taking with them the younger experiments of the plant world.

We learned that ferns and horsetails are not the only primitives lurking in the damp shadows at the edge of the alders. We discovered a pair of Virginia rails—secretive birds whose lineage dates from 70 million years ago—nesting among the cattails, and there were tree frogs, red-legged frogs, and newts in the sedge-choked watery hollows. Living with them were dragonfly nymphs. As the spring days lengthened, the adults began to emerge, spreading their transparent wings into the breeze with time-tested certainty, for long ago their ancestors were among the first flying creatures to arise from the face of the earth.

The marsh stays wet the year around. It is fed by underground water that wells up through the valley alluvium, water from winter rains held back in the uplifted, folded, spongelike coastal hills that cradle the canyons. The canyon in which we live has numerous springs, which slowly feed the stream even in the driest part of summer. It is from this stream that we take our supply of water.

For a long time we were so busy with a new baby and the immediate problems of living that the canyon remained a dark, mist-shrouded secret, luring but inaccessible. One weekend our friend Jonathan was visiting, and the two of us set out to find the source of the stream.

We struck off along one of the upper ridges, assuming that it would be easier to work down rather than up the narrow defile. We rose higher and higher along the steep ascent of the ridge until the lagoon lay far below us, gleaming in the morning sun like a jewel set into the winding coastline. Finally we came to the edge of the grassland and began struggling through dense forest and undergrowth, sometimes crawling on hands and knees. Soon we were in the chaparral, fighting around and under the tough shrubs. The chaparral is another world, above and apart from the cool forest of slopes and canyon. We struggled against the heat, pushing on across the rocky, sunbaked ridge as quickly as the brush would allow.

We finally reached the crest of the ridge and rested beneath a large oak. When we had our fill of the cool Pacific breeze, we found a depression on the forested slope that we thought might be the beginning of our canyon. It was a soft beginning. There was no running water, not even a creek bed, just a gently sloping basin of redwoods carpeted with a deep mat of decaying leaves and occasional ferns.

Then all at once the land made the plunge. The slopes flung themselves up around us and became mighty walls of rock and scree. Bay trees and oaks arched out from their stony strongholds, covering the chasm with a roof of green. There the stream began, small at first, seeping from the spongy ground beneath a cluster of redwoods, then gathering imperceptibly from myriad unseen pores of the sponge until we were slipping and sliding over water-worn boulders and shouting above the din of a hundred little cascades. Five-finger and maidenhair ferns hung from the cliffs, and great primeval fronds of California aralia, some ten feet tall, arched over our heads.

The canyon grew dark and foreboding. Now and then we found ourselves standing among redwoods, huge fire-scarred trunks lifting their needles into the light but leaving little for the ferns beneath them. At other times we scrambled through the tangled branches of bay trees fallen from the steep canyon walls, victims of heavy rains and relentless erosion. All the while the stream was growing, splashing over somber grey sandstone and highly polished roots of the redwoods, as we slithered along with it into the shadows below.

We paused to drink in a small level spot that harbored a quiet pool. Here we discovered a Pacific giant salamander walking near the stream. Nearly a foot long, this is the largest salamander in our region, and we marveled at its beautiful mottled coloration. In this same place, as we stooped to drink from the pool, we found a number of dusky salamander larvae on the bottom, so well camouflaged that only the occasional movement of their feathery external gills revealed their presence.

After much scrambling, wet and tired, we finally came upon the little check dam in the creek, the storage tank, and the pipe that brings water to the ranch yard. In a few more minutes we were walking beneath the giant alders, where the stream was quiet and alder catkins covered the pools like rafts of golden caterpillars. Big white umbels of cow parsnip reached above us toward the mottled alder ceiling. We were relieved that at last the landscape was gentle again, but we knew also that the wild canyon behind us had become part of us and that we would forever be that much changed.

For a week or more at a time, during California summers, inland valleys may be scorched by temperatures that hover around 100°. Along the coast the days are clear and moderate for a time, but then, as hot inland air masses begin to rise, cool Pacific air moves in to fill the void. The breeze stiffens, and from beyond the crashing surf comes a cold, ominous, rolling wall of fog. At times the fog moves in only at night and pulls back again in midmorning, lurking just beyond the breakers, lending its damp chill even while the sun shines. At other times it rolls relentlessly all the way across the Central Valley to the foothills of the Sierra, gripping the land in a cool gray shroud for several days before the sun drives it back to the sea once more.

For most living things in our canyon, these wet fogs bring welcome relief from the long summer drought. Lizards come out to drink the beaded moisture. Forest trees gather the mist until it drips from their leaves as a steady rain, nurturing the ferns that thrive beneath them. But for the swallows these occasional drizzles mean difficult times. The salty mud of their nests crumbles; eggs and babies crash to the ground. If dense fog persists, insects cease to fly, parents go hungry, and additional young die of starvation. As the sun returns, however, the nests are built anew and are soon filled again with hungry, gaping mouths.

Of all places in the canyon, the marsh is the most magically transformed by heavy fog. Spider webs suddenly appear everywhere, made visible by decorations of water droplets. Every blade of sedge and cattail, every stalk of velvet grass and horsetail, equally adorned, adds to the metamorphosis of the landscape.

The marsh is just as beautiful on mornings when the sky is clear and the sun breaks over the ridge-crest trees, illuminating the droplets of dew that accumulated during the cool coastal night. On such mornings it is not the spider webs but the horsetails that reign over the magic kingdom of the marsh. They stand up from the tangled growth like miniature Christmas trees, and from the tips of all their branchlets hang drops of water.

In the summer the marsh is at its best. The ferns are full and green, the alders heavy with leaf. The little ponds we dug as teaching areas teem with life. Cattails tower over us, pushing up their green flower spikes and shedding golden pollen into the wind. Among their stalks the redwing blackbirds nest, the males flashing brilliant shoulder patches in territorial display. For many weeks we revel in the metallic ring of their calls.

To our supreme delight, we found during our first summer that a pair of red-tailed hawks and a pair of great horned owls both nest in the canyon. As our second summer approached, we took careful note of their behavior. When the young were ready to leave the nest, the hawks by day and the owls by night would fly across the canyon to an old fir tree at the edge of the rodent-rich grassland. A great chorus would then ensue, the parents calling and the young answering as fledglings were coaxed to leave the nest to search for food.

As Maggie, Pippin, Bo, and I slept out under an enormous, aged buckeye tree near the house those warm summer evenings, the owls whistled and hooted. Sleep was always much delayed, and not unpleasantly so, by these eerie conversations of the night. We lay for hours looking up into the arching limbs above us, following with our ears what our eyes could not see. Once in a while the owl chorus was joined by an even stranger sound, not quite a bark, not quite a howl, but something unearthly and beyond the ability of language to describe. It could have been the call of a grey fox or a bobcat, for both reside in the canyon.

The bobcats are secretive and by day stay well hidden in the depths of the canyon. We have seldom seen them, but we follow their activities by the scat they leave along the trails. One summer day of record-breaking heat, I was treated to a rare encounter with a bobcat. Late in the afternoon, on my return from errands in town, I entered the driveway just as a bobcat bounded out in front of me. Apparently leaving a drinking place in the marsh hollows, he walked steadily up the drive, his tawny mottled fur glistening in the sun. Without the least concern, he finally turned, looked at me with his soft feline eyes, and loped on into the brush.

Our second summer, like the first one, vanished quickly. It was the busiest time of the year as we watered, harvested, and planted crops for the winter garden. Between the spells of fog, the sun blazed and the cicadas buzzed. The stream dwindled to a soft trickle in the deep canyon and sank beneath the gravel farther down toward the ranch yard. The grass had long since turned brown. Delicate ringlet butterflies flitted through the fields.

The young herons and egrets had left their nests and were learning to feed in the lagoon. Late in the summer, before their departure for the south, many of them began roosting in our canyon. Now and then a dozen birds at a time would rise from their perches, soar above the canyon, then falter in the strong sea winds. Necks and legs outstretched, they would dip and swoop like kites in distress, until they again regained the safety of their roosting trees. Once the afternoon winds had died, the great birds would try again, heading across the ridge for the next canyon and the rookery.

In September the monarch butterflies began to arrive in large numbers, drifting through the canyon on gentle breezes like blowing leaves. Streaming toward the coast from many hundreds of miles away, they would soon gather by the tens of thousands to winter in protected groves of trees set aside by Audubon Canyon Ranch as monarch sanctuaries. One or two generations removed from the breeding grounds, these offspring had never been to the groves before; yet somehow they find them, and they gather in great clusters among the trees, which give them shelter from winter storms. Until the first cold weather, however, they glide about in search of the last flowers, tanking up on the nectar that must sustain them until some warm spell offers a brief break in their long hibernation.

California summers are tenacious in their hold upon the land. Trees are slow to lose their leaves, and warmth persists even after the first rain. Balmy Indian summer days are the most beautiful of the year along the coast; the air is calm, the surf quiet. The fogbanks no longer form, and the sun is hot upon the hillsides. It is the last quiet before the storm.

Our first winter at the Ranch had been a record dry one. Scarcely enough rain fell to wash the leaves from the stream channel. The second season promised to be different. The first rain arrived earlier than usual, and it was heavy. After months of dryness, rain was an indescribable relief. The aroma of that first storm was the smell of the earth reviving, seeds swelling, and fungi coming alive beneath wet leaves. It filled even the house with a sense of well-being.

Indian summer seemed abbreviated, for soon the rains returned in earnest, and the chill that came with them brought color to the big-leaf maples and aralias along the stream, and to wild blackberries and sedges in the marsh. The swallows had left on their long flight south, the monarchs had retreated to their winter groves, and millions of ladybird beetles had gathered deep in the forest to hibernate among fallen limbs. The canyon seemed still and empty, waiting.

Nevertheless, there was plenty of activity to be seen in some quarters. Most of the herons and egrets, and a flock of six hundred brown pelicans that had been feeding in the area during the last weeks of summer, had abandoned the lagoon and headed south. In their wake now came thousands of pintails, mallards, canvasbacks, ruddy ducks, buffleheads, scoters, and numerous other migrant waterfowl. Feeding along the tidal channels and mud flats were great flocks of willets, sandpipers, avocets, curlews, and other wading birds. Here they would spend the winter; the lagoon was carpeted with them, forever bustling with avian activity.

Meanwhile, right outside the windows of the house another function of autumn was developing. Rutting season had arrived among the mule deer. The herd of about fourteen deer that permanently occupies the floor of the canyon consists of numerous females, yearlings, and one or two young bucks. Each spring we are treated to the sight of several tiny fawns nursing in the ranch yard or leaping about in graceful play. But no event in the life of the mule deer is quite as amazing to behold as the time of rut.

As the females one by one come into heat, big bucks from the hills come down and join the herd. These are not the deer that wander fearlessly among us all year, stealing apples from my boxes even while I am on the ladder picking them. These bucks are enormous, alert, wild creatures with great, spreading antlers. Their necks are thick and their bodies muscular. Their carriage is stately; they stalk through the ranch yard like members of visiting royalty.

The bucks spend some time browsing quietly with the herd, but in the fall food is of little object. For the most part, they are busy chasing away the younger males or sniffing along after the does, heads lowered, nostrils expanded. Now and then a buck singles one female from the herd and pursues her relentlessly through the brush until she yields.

More rains fell, and soon the woods and forest were richly endowed with mushrooms, snails, and huge ocher banana slugs. In the grassland golden and banded garden spiders were abundant, their orb webs glistening with drops of water. The marsh had its own complement of spiders, the most beautiful of which were the huge shamrock orb weavers, found only along the coastline.

It was a glorious autumn, wet but mild, and we went with Pippin on many walks around the canyon, taking in the sights and smells. Then suddenly, on December 7, winter arrived with a blast, unlike anything felt in California for decades. A mass of cold air moving south from Alaska brought thermometers plummeting to record lows. Rain turned to hail, and then to snow. For ten straight days the temperature never rose above freezing, and at night it dropped to 15°, 11°, even 8°. Had we been living on the blizzard-swept plains of South Dakota or in

the valleys of Vermont, we would have thought such days were mild. But in California a freeze is another matter. Every hardware store in town ran out of water pipe; service stations placed rush orders for antifreeze, and then there were the unfortunate gardens.

Camellias were wrapped in blankets, fuchsias were covered with pillowcases, jade plants melted in doorways, and sprinklers ran all night in courtyards and patios until icicles hung like the winter facade of Niagara Falls. Everyone with any stake in a eucalyptus tree stood sadly by as the old giant drooped and browned in the frost.

One great lesson was learned by all: "mild coastal weather" and "average temperatures" mean nothing in terms of survival. The distribution of plants on this earth is determined not by averages but by extremes—the hottest summer day, the coldest winter night, the heaviest rain, the longest drought. Our garden plants are exotic captives that understand in their genes the climate extremes of their homelands but know nothing of the extremes in California.

At the Ranch we lost a few fern plants around the house and the vegetable garden, but the larger garden—the coastal scrub, the forest, and the marsh—laughed at the cold. Only the fronds of the bracken ferns were burned, and new ones appeared a week later.

Still, it was a brutal time. Thousands of monarch butterflies perished in their usually protected groves. Icy fog and winds up to fifty miles an hour raged down the canyons and across the lagoon. The goats huddled together for warmth in their shelters. The freezing blasts penetrated every tiny crack in the old ranch house, and the Franklin stove was stoked continuously full with wood.

One morning before sunrise Maggie, Pippin, and I took a long walk along the edge of the lagoon. The shoreline was white with drifts of hail, and behind us the long ridge of Mount Tamalpais was mantled with snow. The night had been so cold that even the salt marsh froze. The mud flats were coated with ice, the marsh plants brittle with frost. As the tide came in, sheets of ice floated on the salt water like miniature bergs.

The arctic weather finally dissipated, warm rains returned, interspersed with fleeting moments of sunshine. We continued our walks, watching the sunlight and cloud shadows work their magic dance among the naked alders, willows, and the spreading limbs of the Great Buckeye, as we had come to call the venerable giant beneath which we had slept during the summer.

Occasionally at sunset the winter sky would blaze a dozen different shades of orange, red, and purple. Some evenings the tide was high and the whole lagoon caught the light like a basin of molten metal; at other times, when the tide was low, only the channels remained, snaking like phosphorescent serpents across the dark mud flats. In these brief instants we felt transported deep within ourselves where the unconscious alone knows of the psychic origins of man, the ancient reaching out of the spirit to embrace the sun. These were not moments for the intellect; they were moments for the soul.

We had an unusual number of spectacular sunsets that winter, and they often prefaced storms. Three storms in succession tore at the coastline. Trees fell, and mud slides ripped down from the canyon walls. It was a wild time, but these fierce January storms broke the back of winter. From then on, spring slowly gained control of the land.

The first wild flowers had already appeared in the forest. White milkmaids, purple trillium, and stalks of blue hound's-tongue reached up from the damp carpet of leaves, and the strange orchidlike blossoms of fetid adder's-tongue appeared beneath the redwoods.

Of these January flowers, the adder's-tongue lilies particularly attracted our attention. We wondered why the flowers were greenish-brown rather than some bright color, and why they emitted the strong, musty odor from which the description "fetid" is derived. In all the time we spent at the blossoms watching for insect pollinators, the only

visitors were fungus gnats, known for their attraction to food by smell rather than sight. We concluded that this peculiar insect-flower relationship had evolved because in the dimly lit forest of midwinter bees, butterflies, and other pollinators that are attracted by bright colors are not present. The adder's-tongue has developed a system to utilize the services of one of the only insect species available at that time of year.

As we studied the development of the plants, we were also struck by the fact that almost immediately after blooming, the flower stems elongated and curled downward to the ground. There among the fallen leaves the seed pods formed. We never saw them dry and open to shed their seeds. Instead, as the pods swelled to maturity, some small creatures of the forest chewed them open and took the seeds.

Pursuing this problem in the literature, Maggie and I learned that the seeds of the adder's-tongue are accompanied by attached fatty structures, known as aliosomes, that are especially attractive to ants. Seeds or pods, which are hooked or barbed for dispersal by fur-bearing animals, are borne on upright stalks so that a passing mammal may brush against them; but the stalks of the adder's-tongue bend to the ground instead so that the ants might more easily find the seeds. They chew into the pods, carry the seeds off toward their nest, and at some point along the way may chew the aliosomes from them to lighten their burden. If the seeds are left behind an inch, a yard, or several yards from the parent plant, dispersal has been accomplished.

Scarcely had the last fierce winds of the storm subsided before the buds burst on the willows, revealing silver catkins which soon opened for the business of pollination. By the first week of February, the huge leaf buds of the buckeye trees were opening. More wild flowers, more leaves, taller grass, and soon winter was little more than a memory and a few scars.

Over the past three years of hiking, exploring, and sharing as a family our feelings and the joys of discovery, we have begun to know this small piece of coastal California. We have become acquainted with events of the seasons, familiar with many plants and animals that live near us, and aware, above all, of the peace and spiritual fulfillment we have gained from our natural surroundings.

Thus we have spent our free moments, but the search for a means of living that does not violate the principles, the beauty, and the spirit of this world has occupied most of our time.

Planting the Seeds

As the very act of daily living has occupied an increasing number of our days, we have had to define the intangible value of time as opposed to the established value of money, its modern equivalent. In so doing, we have become more selective in our choice of work and more aware of the delicate balance between our need for solitude and our need for human contact.

Through the joys and trials of searching for the meaning of "family," we have grown closer as a family unit, and we have learned also that the creatures that share the canyon with us are all part of the larger family to which man belongs.

The beauty of exploring a wild place with young children is that they are less interested in the destination than in the things they find along the way. Pippin slowed our pace and opened our eyes with his keen perception. Poppies and butterflies, maples and redwoods could no longer be taken for granted. We began to see them as part of a new world to be shared together.

Maggie and I had learned a little about cattails from our studies. We knew that the evolution of tiny windborne seeds, produced by the thousands on each stalk, increased the odds of dispersal to distant ponds. But it was the child in us rather than the biologist who remembered the joy of bursting cattails, and this joy we found again with Pippin.

Establishing a garden where none had existed was at first like stark pioneering. Year by year the plots were extended; rocks were removed from the canyon alluvium, and fresh produce began to flow from the rich earth. Soon trips to the store dwindled to just a few a year.

*The transformation of a handful of seeds into a year's
supply of food through the ancient alliance between leaf
and sun is a miracle that has fascinated man since the
dawn of agriculture. To know the source of one's
sustenance and to share in the labor of its production are
components of our age-old link with the soil. This, we
decided, must be part of the heritage we pass on to
our son.*

Unique in man is the ability to appreciate plants not simply as food but also as aggregations of form, color, and texture that evoke in the spirit a sense of beauty. The thrill of the harvest comes from more than our basic need to eat and so also does the satisfaction we gain from combining these magnificent forms and flavors in a spontaneous, creative meal.

Raising goats began innocently enough. We wanted fresh milk, cheese, and yogurt for the table, and manure for the garden; we also wanted to share as a family in the birth of new life. But as the herd began to multiply, the second and most difficult half of husbandry loomed before us: the taking of a life to sustain our own.

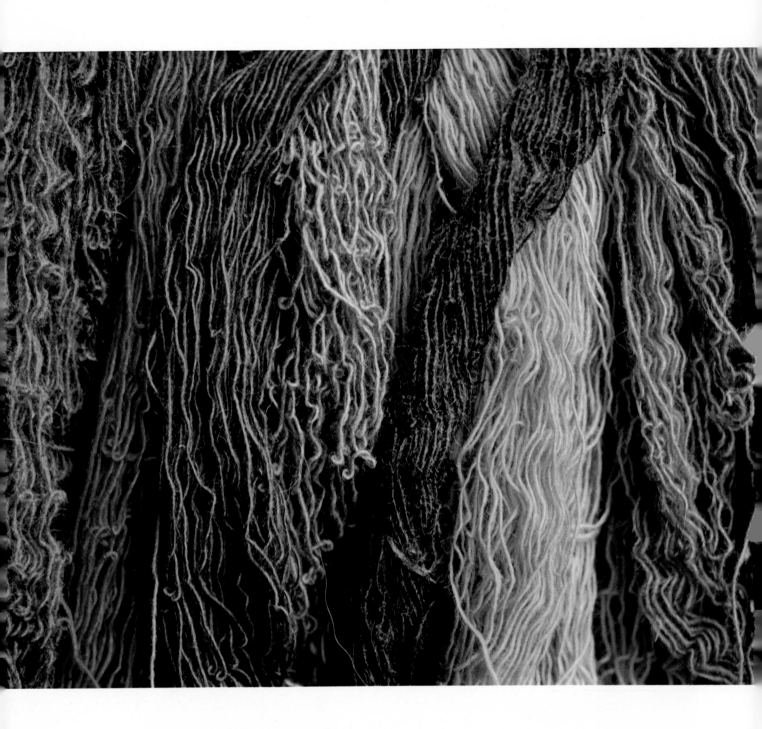

Maggie learned to spin wool and dye the yarn with colors
brewed from plants, many of which she grew in the garden
or collected in the hills.

Stocking caps and weavings were made with the yarn she spun from sheep, goat, and dog hair.

*As the bees in our hives filled their cells with honey and
with pollen of many colors, we learned about another miracle
of the natural world.*

From the garden as a whole, complete with its bees, its pests, and their
various predators and parasites, we observed also the relationship
between our human food web and those that prevail in the wilds
around us. In learning to do things for ourselves, with our own hands
and our own energy, we realized by sheer contrast the immense energy
needed to support modern agriculture and current levels of consumption. By living more simply without, we began to feel a certain peace,
simplicity, and satisfaction within.

2

SUBSISTENCE

For a number of years a deepening concern had been welling up within us over the materialistic, highly consumptive, often environmentally destructive way of life that has gradually gained dominance in every industrial country of the world. As a result, we began teaching children, sharing with others an understanding of ecology and a sense of the beauty of the natural world. We joined conservation organizations and exercised our right to vote in the hope of influencing those we thought responsible for the damage being done to the environment. And then a memory arose of something my father had once said many years before. He had expressed the belief that a person makes his greatest contribution to the world through the way in which he leads his life. Gradually our environmental concerns began no longer to appear as someone else's responsibility alone. We, too, were part of the unbalanced flock, plundering the planet in the very innocence of living itself.

A single powerful desire took form within us: to do in actuality what for most Americans had become only a nostalgic memory—to restore a sense of joy, meaning, spiritual satisfaction, and ecological balance to the act of daily living.

The concern behind our frustration and desire for change was intellectual. But the conscious side of man floats like a thin film over a vast, dark inner flow, seldom explored and little understood. It is the realm of the unconscious that gives foundation to our feelings and life to our spirits. It is the unconscious that emerges from the far, dim past of our species and speaks to us of our heritage. It was primarily this mysterious force within us that drove us back toward the simple life.

Long before we were consciously aware of it, our unconscious had been shaping our responses. This was the source of our uneasiness over a hectic way of life. This was the source of the satisfaction and joy we felt when we cooked a good meal or put in a hard day of manual labor working the soil in our little garden and tending the plants for our table.

It was not until we moved to the Ranch, however, and began the task of sustaining ourselves primarily through our own direct efforts that this ancient calling surfaced. Only when the job became a daily affair did the unconscious begin to reveal its true hold upon us, for such is the power of our age-old link with the land.

On the porch of our San Geronimo Valley cabin, flats of spring vegetable seedlings were waiting for moving day. We had chosen our garden plot at the Ranch carefully so that it would receive maximum sunlight, be reasonably close to the house, yet not encroach upon significant wild places that we knew would prove valuable as teaching areas. We had also planned the garden so that it would be adjacent to a rocky slope where goats could be housed without becoming winter-mired in mud. Through this proximity garden discards could be efficiently fed to the animals and manure piled to compost close to the plots that would later receive it.

This plan left only the most important matter of soil to consider. The floor of the entire valley had been built from coarse alluvium washed out of the canyon. The soil everywhere was therefore laced with gravel, but in the proposed area it was also deep and rich from years of use as a livestock holding area when the canyon last functioned as a subsistence farm. We concluded that we must take the blessing of good soil along with the curse of rocks, and so a week before moving we began to prepare the garden.

Since the goats would have to be moved with us, building a shed and pen were the first jobs on the agenda. A friend came to help, and we set to work, first on a double shed and then on the pen itself, separated down the middle by a fence, one side for Snowballs and the other for Sunflower. Neither of us had constructed anything much beyond shelving before. No corners met quite on the perpendicular, and none of the fence posts remained fully vertical as we stretched the fence wire, but when we had finished, no words could describe our feelings of accomplishment.

More friends and members of the family came another day to help with the deer fence around the garden. Once the selected area was enclosed, I started in on the soil. The first turning was made with a heavy-duty tiller, for the bunch grasses were tough and the river rocks more numerous than we had anticipated.

The tilling completed, I began to work the soil by hand, prying stone after stone from the tangled grass roots. I was alone now in the canyon; Maggie was making final preparations for moving. The wind moaned through the fence wire. Its mournful sound stirred visions of the lonely prairie in my imagination. Nature had firmly reclaimed this place where once a farm had been, and the tasks before us seemed like stark pioneering. From this rocky soil we would take our sustenance.

The first few plots were planted immediately after we moved to the Ranch so that we would have a steady supply of homegrown food while Maggie nursed Pippin during his first year of life. Maggie joined me in the garden, and plot by plot, the soil was carefully prepared. To save hauling, the tons upon tons of rock we removed from the soil were placed as pavement upon the paths, and thus the curse we feared became, with immense effort, another blessing.

It took us two years to complete the garden and a third to prepare an extension. Sustenance did begin to flow from the rocky soil in plenty. This sustenance, however, was made possible by one single basic ingredient: consistent, hard, often back-breaking work. I remembered a number of community gardens we had watched spring up near our former place of residence. Groups of young people had banded together in some vacant lot or spare field with the intention of growing wholesome, clean, sweet country food. They scratched some seeds into the ground, dashed a bit of water on them now and then, and sat back waiting, talking philosophy on the fence rails. They got a few stunted radishes and the inevitable zucchini, but usually by the second season the fields lay fallow, save some very healthy weeds. No, it takes more than philosophy to start a garden.

The initial burden we inherited from the soil, however, was more than compensated for by the available water. The first settlers, and the Indians before them who had for untold generations used the canyon as an encampment, took their water from this stream. Forty years ago the present gravity-fed water system was installed. Except for times of big storms every few years, when the stream is laden with silt, the water flows each day crystal clear and cold to the old ranch house. When I drink this spring water, I sometimes think of the minerals it contains—bits and pieces of the towering ridge behind us—and all that the water has experienced in the gouging of this and who-knows-how-many other canyons on the face of the earth. I sometimes think that I can taste the legacy of this water, for it comes to us pure out of the ground and has not, in its short residency here, known the befouling hand of man. Once in a while, when the screens fail, sticks, leaves, or water beetles emerge unexpectedly from the tap, but we simply accept them as part of the inheritance.

It is this water, too, which flows in abundance to the vegetable garden. During the first spring and summer we spent long days together among the plots, shucking rocks from the soil, weeding, watering, and nurturing the crops we had planted. From his very first days, Pippin joined us, cuddled peacefully among the squash vines while the sun shone down upon him and the leaves rustled in the coastal breeze. Now and then Sunflower the goat and our rapidly growing buck would speak to us reproachfully about the greening of the plots until we would throw some garden tidbits over the fence.

If Sunflower, through the easy birth of her first two kids, has given us our first lessons concerning the innate behavior of domesticated animals, Snowballs the billy goat impressed them indelibly upon us. Sunflower was at least subtle. She worked upon our minds. Snowballs' influence, however, was felt almost entirely through the seat of our pants.

When we first obtained him from friends, Snowballs was no larger than an average-sized dog. In order to mate with Sunflower, he was obliged to stand on a log. But five months later when Tinga and Sienna were born, he had already become an enormous creature, and he was still growing. His neck thickened and his horns grew long and sturdy. He strutted around his pen with complete confidence; His Lordship the harem master was in command.

Snowballs and I had our first major difference of opinion about fences. We had made the unfortunate mistake of building his pen adjacent to the does in order to have both goat houses under the same roof. We had traded Tinga as payment for the buck and then bred Sunflower when she first came into heat in the fall. As soon as Sienna was ready for breeding, however, Snowballs simply hooked the fencing with his horns and removed it forthwith. Our plans to breed Sienna in the spring so that the milk flow would be prolonged over more months met instant demise, and I set about rebuilding the fence.

The noble beast tormented me endlessly. He stole my hat, pulled out and chewed my shirttail, and repeatedly tipped over the can of fencing staples. He made numerous false charges, rearing high on his hind legs and coming at me with head lowered, but always, he stopped short of his mark. I knew these antics to be bluff, and I tried very hard to ignore him. I had nearly finished the fence repairs when for an instant I turned my glance away from him. With a blow to both my backside and my sense of authority that I can feel to this day, Snowballs sent me headlong through the fence I had so carefully replaced. As manager of the herd, I was forced to admit, I had definitely failed my first test.

Maggie, who had assumed most of the tasks of tending the goats, steadfastly refused to deal with Snowballs. But she was left alone with him one day when I was running errands in town. I had just arrived for lunch at the house of a friend when the phone rang. It was Maggie.

She reported, somewhat out of breath, that Snowballs had broken the fence and had penned half a dozen Audubon ladies in the longhouse. She had called in a neighbor who came to the rescue with a quickly fastened lasso.

"Where is he now?" I ventured.

"Up on the hill, all tangled in poison oak."

I rushed home as quickly as I could negotiate the winding country roads. With apprehension I approached the house. All was quiet and Snowballs was in his pen.

"How did you get him back?" I asked her in amazement.

Maggie smiled and replied casually, "Oh, I just grabbed him by the horns and walked him back."

During our first summer the garden prospered. Laced with organic matter and lots of manure, the newly worked soil responded in kind to our labors. Out of one tiny patch in which Maggie had planted potatoes, she dug 160 pounds of tubers. The largest single head of broccoli weighed five pounds. We had tomatoes weighing a pound and a quarter, ten-pound cabbages and cauliflowers, seven-pound ruta-bagas, and sweet Italian red onions that *averaged* a pound apiece! One small paper bag of Jerusalem artichoke tubers multiplied to fill a heavy-duty garden wheelbarrow twice. We did not go hungry, nor did our friends and neighbors.

By midsummer plots vacated by early crops were filled with plantings for the winter. As the days grew shorter and rains and frosts returned, we feasted upon a continuous supply of root crops, greens, and other morsels from the garden, blending them with winter squash, potatoes, onions, and other items we had placed in storage.

Winter chores and teaching kept us busy at the Ranch. Spring returned swiftly, and we made ready for the birth of a new crop of goats.

We had tied Sunflower out for some fresh greens one morning while I raked apple tree prunings from the grass nearby. Suddenly I heard a grunt and turned toward the goat. Seeing that she was in labor, I rushed to the house to call Maggie and fetch the camera. We were back in less than five minutes, Pippin and Bo in tow, but the first kid had already been born. Sunflower was lying on the ground, gently licking the membranes from a tan male with snow flecks and long white ears.

Within fifteen minutes a second kid emerged, feet first, nose nestled between its knees, a mere shadow of mammalian form emersed in fluid and encased by the translucent amniotic sac. Within a few seconds the little goat kicked open the sac and gasped for breath. Sunflower went instantly to work removing the wrappings. In less than five minutes a tiny cinnamon-colored female stood before us on wobbly legs while its mother tenderly cleaned its fur and chewed off the extra length of umbilical cord. She would be the third milk goat in the herd, and we named her Amber.

Assuming that the birthing had been completed, we were occupied with the firstborn, which had already taken its first drink of milk and was busy playing with Pippin, when suddenly a third baby appeared upon the scene. Another male, mostly black with brown ears. We named him Fig and his brother Fog.

Pippin was ecstatic. He crawled in and out among the goats, pulling tails and umbilical cords, tugging on ears, and patting heads while the three kids romped and played, probed and suckled. Sunflower bleated softly in reassuring tones, and Bo, with wrinkled brow, hovered over the entire operation like a proud and concerned father. Meanwhile, Snowballs, who was also staked out in the grass nearby, grazed on with detached disinterest. He had done his part and seemed perfectly content to leave the rest of the fathering to the dog.

Once the flurry of excitement had passed, Maggie and I sat quietly in the grass watching Pippin as he made acquaintance with these new members of our extended family. What an amazing process, this ungulate system of birth! All during the winter, while the caterpillars, ladybird beetles, and monarchs were hibernating, while the trees stood dormant and the frigid storm winds raged, these tiny sparks of life had been growing in the watery warmth of the womb. They had felt no frost and heard no storm. Only the steady beat of Sunflower's heart had penetrated their protected world. For five months they had slowly grown, in dark and warm security, and then suddenly this. Within five minutes of their abrupt emergence into the spring sun they were standing; in five more minutes they were nursing, and before another five had passed they were playing!

How different it had been with Pippin. Born the same size as Amber, for long months he hung from Maggie's shoulders, wrapped in a cloth. He slowly learned first to creep and then to crawl. Now he was a year old and not yet quite as adept physically as these newborn kids. But the mind of a human child is another matter. We watched as Pippin explored these new creatures with his hands and extended his emotions openly toward them. What had been developing in that infant mind while the body remained dependent upon parental attention, and what potential remained? As they played together, Pippin and his hooved companions seemed as close in their heritage as brothers and

yet the distance of potential stretched wide between them.

The next day Maggie recorded every stage of the event in our farm and garden journal. She concluded with the following entry:

"Twenty hours after the birth I took all three to the astonished postmaster at Stinson Beach. In exchange for a loaf of pumpkin bread, she weighed them in as follows: Fog, 9 lbs.; Fig, 7½ lbs.; Amber, 6½ lbs.—23 pounds of live kid goat."

We were not long in discovering the simple mathematics of goat-raising: with two teats on one side and three mouths on the other, the equation simply did not balance. Sunflower knew this without any lessons in algebra, and within a short time she had rejected Amber, the smallest of the three. Though her milk supply was adequate for all, once again the ancient instincts had surfaced, and we knew that bottle feeding would now be added to our daily chores. Sunflower allowed Maggie to act as an intermediary and gave her extra milk freely.

Maggie checked the journal to calculate when Sienna would give birth. On the predicted day a single male kid appeared in the pen and was soon running at Sienna's side. As the young goats grew, Sienna also shared some of her milk for Amber's bottle.

The farm and garden journal provided us with information far beyond the affairs of the goats. Ever since my earliest interest in natural history and gardening, I had been advised by parents, teachers, and friends of the importance of keeping a journal. I started one once when I was studying biology in high school, but soon enough I gave it up as a tedious collection of miscellany. For years I resisted, but Maggie had taken the idea more seriously during her college field work. When we first came to the Ranch, knowing that we would be deeply involved in teaching, Maggie suggested that we begin a series of journals dealing with various aspects of natural history in which we and the students could enter our observations. Because we thought that the garden might in some way play a role in our teaching, we threw in an extra book to cover this endeavor as well. We had little idea at the time how significant Maggie's intuition was and how valuable this and the other journals would prove to be.

During the first year we simply entered the garden events chronologically. Every planting and transplanting, and the beginning and end of each harvest were duly recorded. Occasional observations about the health of the crops or problems with pests were entered as well, and maps were drawn for the purpose of noting crop rotation. In some cases we kept track of total yield per square foot of garden space in order to assess on a comparative basis the actual productivity of certain crops. As time went on, I could see that some interesting information was developing, but since time was precious, keeping up with the journal still appeared to me to be a rather unnecessary added chore.

I had been growing vegetables off and on since I was a child. I had worked side by side with my grandfather and my father, and I had learned much from their accumulated experience. I had observed my own successes and failures carefully and made adjustments in techniques accordingly. Occasional problems aside, I had come to assume that I had things pretty well in hand, for my gardens were always more than ample.

Nevertheless, when a full year of records had accumulated, I sat down with the journal and began to extract and organize the data. Here before me emerged an amazing body of helpful information. I began to see numerous places for the improvement of planting and cultivation techniques.

Very much humbled from my discoveries, I set about devising ways of making the data more graphic to facilitate clearer interpretation and easier

keeping of records. Most valuable of all was a simple graph that I developed for the comparative recording, year after year, of planting, transplanting, and harvesting information. By making three or four quick marks during the season for each crop, we would have a graphic illustration of most of the facts, processes, and characteristics we would need to arrive at a reasonably accurate assessment of our successes and failures.

During the second year of gardening at the Ranch, we kept our records judiciously and began to make adjustments in our approach to some of the problems we had encountered.

We had feared difficulty in growing crops in the cool coastal climate, but our experience was far more encouraging than we had anticipated. The canyon proved to be reasonably sheltered from summer fog winds. Even when the fog settled in for a week at a time, the weather remained mild. We quickly learned that growing hot-weather crops such as melons, peppers, and eggplant was out of the question, but we were pleased that in spite of cool summers we could manage fine, if somewhat delayed, crops of corn and tomatoes. Furthermore, we were delighted to discover that lettuce, cauliflower, cabbage, peas, and a variety of other cool-weather crops could be grown with outstanding results all summer. Tempered by the thermostatic

effect of the Pacific Ocean, the winters were so mild that we were able to keep an abundance of fresh food growing all winter long.

Very quickly we fell into a pattern of seasonal crop rotation that involved forty basic kinds of vegetables and no less than one hundred twenty different varieties. With this kind of diversity facing us each year, the garden records gained immensely in importance.

Concerning pests, our experience gave us far more cause for concern. During the first summer we had very few insect problems. We attributed this fact to the garden's wilderness setting. Surrounded by a reasonably balanced natural ecosystem, we reasoned, the garden would be kept fairly free of pest species by a diversity of parasites and predators. On the other hand, we anticipated more problems with the larger wildlife than we had experienced in former gardens we had tended in town.

We did have the deer fence, which proved essential, but we had little defense against a flock of thirty-two quail, numerous other birds that came to eat the seedlings and berries, and raccoons and foxes that made nocturnal raids once in a while in search of tasty morsels. After all, we were living in a wildlife sanctuary, and in any case, we were not inclined toward the killing of wildlife. Instead, we learned the seasonal habits of these animals, timed our plantings as best we could to avoid the most damage, and otherwise either protected the crops from them or planted enough to share.

Gophers, moles, deer mice, and meadow mice, however, did so much damage in the garden that we were obliged to control them or give up on many crops entirely. In a sense this policy was only an attempt to maintain the natural balance in an otherwise artificial setting. Protected from usually shy predators by their proximity to human

activity and surrounded by an abundance of food not found in the surrounding wilderness, the rodents rapidly increased in numbers beyond the normal density. We ourselves, therefore, had to substitute for the predators that were largely kept back from the valley by our very presence.

These problems we expected, but the difficulties we were to have with insects took us by surprise after our successes the first year. By the time the second spring and summer rolled around, a host of rather disagreeable companions began to appear in the garden. Leaves were chewed by caterpillars, cucumber beetles, earwigs, snails, and slugs. A new crop of baby slugs in the spring wiped out our entire stand of Chinese cabbage, and every radish, carrot, and cauliflower succumbed as the roots were consumed by fly larvae and millipedes. Soil flatworms and sow bugs took most of the strawberries as they ripened, and cucumber beetle larvae ate the roots of many squash seedlings.

The initial plowing of the garden had destroyed many of the potentially harmful soil creatures, and the insects had not yet discovered the rich bounty, so our first-year crops had been pest-free. It took a full season for their numbers to increase from the population a wild area could support to one that could only be sustained by the exotic domesticates of man.

Our original thesis still held some validity, however. A host of parasites and predators did invade the garden and began their work among the munching, sucking, burrowing hordes. We had birds, lacewings, ladybird beetles, spiders, caterpillar parasites, syrphid fly larvae, soldier beetles, and aphid wasps in abundance by the second year. Native plant-eaters were held in check by these indigenous parasites and predators. Only the introduced pests that had remained in the canyon since the early farming days presented a major threat to our own sustenance.

Because of their dangerous effects upon human health and wildlife, we refused to use any chemical means of pest control. Instead, we gradually developed a variety of new cultivation techniques and physical means of control, which began to show promising results. The most important changes, however, took place in our own attitude. We found that we no longer worried about a certain percentage of loss in the garden, because, even with the loss of a crop or two, there was always more than enough to share. We had learned enough from the natural world to realize that the simple laws of population control could work for us in the garden if only we were patient enough to allow them expression in their own time. Holes in leaves or roots, or aphids in the broccoli indicated to us only that natural laws were being observed rather than violated.

At any rate, these periodic surprises at mealtime could not possibly detract from the pleasure of cooking and eating the garden-fresh produce we had tenderly nurtured from seed to harvest. Maggie had learned certain basics about cooking as a child, and since both my father and mother are talented and creative in the kitchen, I was attracted to the art of cooking long before I left home. By the time we moved to the Ranch, Maggie and I had established a satisfactory rhythm of creative cooking, based in part on the things we grew in our small gardens.

But now we had a much larger area under cultivation. With a vast, year-round assortment of fruits and vegetables, milk from the goats, and our own supply of meat on the way, our immediately available resources had considerably increased. Cooking and gardening continued to be enterprises shared between us, but since I had assumed more of the responsibility for growing the food, Maggie took on a larger share of cooking it.

Above all that we have learned so far in our experience of living close to the land, the transfor-

mation of a handful of seeds into delicious meals, simply and quickly prepared, has emerged as the greatest miracle and most joyful enterprise. The distance in quality between store-bought produce and vegetables picked fresh from the garden only moments before cooking is too vast for words to describe. The satisfaction of eating seasonally brought an even more remarkable change in our attitude toward food. Fresh corn and tomatoes in winter or celeriac in the summer were now not out of the question. Frozen or processed foods no longer found their way to our table, and we no longer relied upon the extravagance of off-season crops from Florida or the Coachella Valley. Since we had not found time to build a fox- and raccoon-proof chicken house, we still purchased eggs, and once in a while during the wintertime we brought a crate of oranges from town. Excepting these items and staples such as honey, salt, flour, dried beans, and grain, we relied upon what we had.

This reliance on the products of our own labor in our own climate had a profound effect upon our cooking. By choice we denied ourselves the luxury of unseasonal fruits and vegetables beyond our own larder. It therefore became nearly impossible to use most cookbooks literally. We could not work backward from recipes to an all-season supermarket produce counter but had to work forward from the garden and pantry themselves. Neither of us had ever relied much on recipes, but now we found that our cooking was becoming even more spontaneous. A few minutes before dinner, we simply went out to the garden, picked what struck our immediate taste or what most needed harvesting, and combined these ingredients with whatever eggs, meat, cheese, staples, or leftovers happened to be on hand. The event of synthesis was always an inspiration and an adventure; dinner usually took only a few minutes to prepare, and the results were seldom anything but superb.

This tradition we adopted and this we continue, not as a chore but as a joyous part of our daily life. We crave the thrill of harvest, the sweet aromas of preparing the food, and the satisfaction of making do with what we have. We have found also that, by eating seasonally, our appreciation of foods has increased. By the time fresh corn is ripe on the stalks or the first vine-ripe tomatoes are ready to pick, months of anticipation renders them even more delicious than they would otherwise be. When apple season, pear season, or persimmon season finally arrives, these fruits seem like the most delectable productions the world has ever known. Maggie commented one day that, at age thirty, she could remember only about twenty-five times in her whole life when she had tasted the first peach of the season or the first apricot. These are rare and precious moments, and they have been all but obliterated by modern marketing techniques.

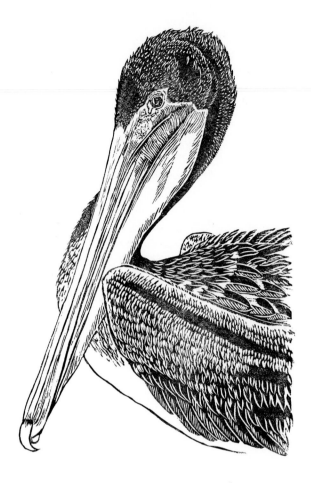

In spite of our growing independence of the supermarket, however, we have not been without reminders of the problems that have resulted from modern agribusiness. As the brown pelicans arrive in Bolinas Lagoon each summer, we have been painfully aware that few juveniles accompany them. For many years, until finally halted by law, DDT discharged into the Los Angeles basin by a single manufacturing plant had been concentrating in the food web and finally in the pelicans, thus disrupting the breeding biology of the Channel Island colony.

On errand days in town Maggie and I often discussed the lack of homegrown food in the large ornamental gardens of the suburbs. One by one, the small, often diversified farms of the past have been replaced by enormous agribusiness corporations, and seemingly endless acreages of single crops have spread across the land. Most of those who used to till the soil themselves have fled to the cities where now they, too, must feed from the hand of the few. In America, roughly 10 percent of our population produces the food consumed by the remaining 90 percent. In China, a nonindustrial nation, the percentages are exactly the reverse.

We have also been concerned about the increasing consumption of energy in modern agriculture. When we grow our own food, we expend a certain amount of energy in the process, but when we eat that food, the energy is replenished with plenty to spare, placed in reserve for other endeavors. This direct cycle involves only us, our animals, the soil and water, the plants, and the sun. By the time commercial food products reach the kitchen, however, they have partaken not only of human energy but also of the immense energy expended by tractors, harvesters, trucks, refrigeration units, processing and packaging plants, the energy used in the manufacture of all this paraphernalia as well as sprays, fertilizers, preservatives, emulsifiers, and colorings, and the energy consumed by secondary distributors and the marketers themselves. By the time it reaches the American kitchen, seven times as much energy has been expended on the average food item as that food itself contains.

Ordering seeds from catalogs advertising the latest hybrids has reminded us of the precarious nature of modern agricultural genetics. Our culture is almost entirely dependent upon food crops which, through constant selection for high yield and disease resistance, are founded upon a decreasing gene pool farther and farther removed from a genetic base that could persist without vigilant, highly mechanized attention. Numerous scientists have warned that the present system of agriculture may become increasingly susceptible to genetic collapse in the face of newly evolving diseases or other environmental factors. In the selection of our own garden crops, therefore, we have settled for the most part upon basic, often old-fashioned varieties from which we can save our own seed, avoiding wherever possible those hybrids that have been unduly inflated by modern genetics.

By breaking away from these perhaps dangerous and certainly unproven trends as much as our small space would allow, we have received a growing sense of independence and increasing satisfaction. The most intense rewards, however, have come from a rediscovery of our ancient connections with the soil. The exhilaration of providing our own sustenance, the sense of challenge we have felt in learning the skills of simple agriculture, and the satisfaction we have experienced from participating in every step of the process have emerged from deep within us.

One lesson we have learned in meeting the daily schedule on our miniature farm is the importance of a reasonable division of labor. The earliest terri-torial banter between Maggie and me developed the first year over the potato patch. In our previous garden Maggie had initiated the growing and harvesting of spuds, and had assumed responsibility for their well-being. As the new garden was being prepared, it became apparent to me that she intended to make good once again her claim to the territory of the tubers, and a certain mild conflict of interest developed over the allotment of space. I conceded one plot, from which she later dug a fine harvest.

Another and larger territorial confrontation developed the second year over the planting of flowers. So precious had been our space and our time the first season that we had not planted flowers. A portion of the garden remained as yet unworked, and both Maggie and I had been eyeing it for future use. We both agreed that we must have some flowers and that we also must have some berry vines. It was only again a matter of relative space. A compromise was reached, and some of both were planted.

Maggie's flowers were indeed a feast for the eye (Pippin's first word for them was "wowers"), but since I was more concerned about a feast for the stomach, I occasionally grumbled about the space they were removing from gastronomic productivity. Then one day Maggie devised so clever a scheme for justifying their presence in the garden that I had to relent. She simply ordered two hive boxes and the honeybees to fill them.

First the hives arrived at the post office, and Maggie assembled and located them. They were soon followed by the bees themselves, three pounds (or 10,000 bees) and a queen for each hive, and once again the postmaster cheerfully cooperated with our peculiar postal traffic. The bees immediately went to work building combs and gathering nectar and pollen among Maggie's flowers.

She studied their activities carefully, noting which varieties they preferred and identifying by color the pollen they were taking back to the hives. This information she added to the garden records so that the following year she would know which flowers to emphasize in her plots for the benefit of the bees. Once the colonies were established, we went together to inspect the hives. I operated the smoker while Maggie worked among the comb frames. We were amazed to discover beautiful patterns of color showing through the backs of the partially filled frames, colors representing the many different kinds of pollen that by chance were added first to the bottom of each cell.

Studying the bees and watching their activities was a fascinating new enterprise. Maggie had completely won me over. We had never been truly serious about our territorial squabbles, but we were gradually learning even more fully the significance and joy of sharing the farm chores. For convenience and efficiency we gradually settled into a certain customary division of labor, but we recognized the importance of knowing the details of each other's tasks. We found as time went on that only by doing each other's work could we fully appreciate each other's efforts, problems, and rewards. The more we have swapped roles, the more common ground we have and the richer our relationship has grown.

The bees, and to a certain extent the goats, have taught us something else of importance. Trial and error alone is not always sufficient in learning a new skill, and it is certainly not necessarily the most efficient way to approach the task at hand. Beekeeping is a highly refined science, and goat-raising has a longer history than that of almost any other domesticated animal. We soon discovered the power of the printed word in conveying the collective wisdom of the past concerning these practical skills.

We began to assemble a library of useful books, and the reading we did concerning bees and goats was invaluable. But the books did not stop with these subjects. Maggie had for some time been interested in edible native plants, and she had already developed some excellent uses for those with which we were familiar. Still, the books she found were most helpful. She made cobblers, pies, and jam from wild blackberries, elderberries, and huckle-

berries; jelly from manzanita berries; tea from madrone bark, yerba buena, and the spring shoots of Douglas fir; bread from the rhizomes of cattails and cookies from their golden pollen; pickles from bull kelp; salads from watercress, wild mustard flowers, and miner's lettuce. She found a dozen ways to incorporate the vitamin-rich stinging nettle into our meals, and as she learned a few easily identified mushrooms, they too became a frequent ingredient in our food.

We found a new level of satisfaction in the wild harvest, one that emerged from an even older stage of human evolution than agriculture. We felt an intensified kinship with the Miwok Indians, who must also have eaten these foods in this very canyon before they met their well-known fate at the hands of our own race. The gathering of acorns in the fall has become for us a minor pilgrimage, as it was for the Indians of California on a far larger and more important scale. It is when we gather mushrooms, however, that the bounty of the land seems to affect us most deeply. There is something in the rich, earthy smell of a basketful of chantrelles or oyster and honey mushrooms that awakens our ancient connections with the wilderness from whose embrace man wandered long ago upon the first planting of a seed.

Through her interest in Indian lore and edible plants, Maggie also became intrigued with the idea of spinning her own yarn and dyeing it with colors brewed from native plants, and once again more informative books were added to our library. It was not long before a spinning wheel occupied the middle of the living room, and in the evening Maggie spun by the hour as we talked, while Pippin stood close by in fascination. Many plants were brewed, and beautiful earth colors penetrated the wool yarn she had spun. Soon decorative weavings, useful caps, and a puffy handcrafted frog for Pippin had been completed during the spare moments of evening.

To the many colors of dyed sheep wool, she added the neatly spun underfur she had combed from the goats as well as the combings from the dogs of many friends. I have a warm feeling when I think of the many animals that have given their fur for the wool cap I wear, the care of their owners in combing and saving it for us, and the time Maggie spent spinning, dyeing, and knitting the final product. In what store-bought cap could one find that kind of legacy?

It was from the enterprise of spinning and dyeing that Maggie first learned about the significance of tools. The wheel itself she purchased as a kit to save time, since spinning wheels are complex to build and the old one in my family had been abandoned when I was still very young. But the accessories she made herself, based upon the plans of the pioneers. With teasel heads, pieces of wood, leather thongs, and stick handles, she fashioned a pair of carders. From a three-pronged branch, she carved a useful distaff upon which to hang her

skeins of yarn. As she began her weavings, she made simple looms, and from pieces of wood and antlers and shoulder blades of deer, she carved a set of magnificent needles, beating combs, and shuttles, derived in part from tools developed by the Navajos.

It was in reading a book on Navajo weaving (*Working with the Wool*, by Noel Bennett and Tiana Bighorse) that Maggie came across these lines: "A good tool is highly valued by Navajo weavers and receives special care. Some are extremely specialized. A weaver usually has favorite ones, whose weight and balance are a part of her. Replacements for these are hard to come by. . . . Some weavers give expression to the power they feel in a tool. To lend a tool to someone is to give of your power. Thus, it is not frequent that a tool is lent or given unless, of course, it is to a close and trusted friend, and then it is not just the loan of a tool, but a gift of energy and ideas as well."

Maggie had discovered in making the carders that they functioned better for her than the commercial designs she had tried, for she had modified them until they fit her hands and the particular way

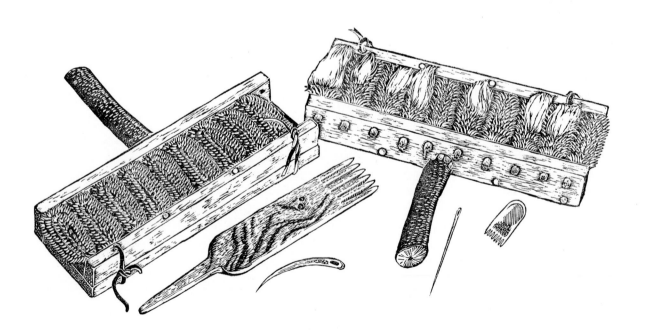

in which she worked the wool. In refining the tools of bone and wood, she developed a respect for them she had never experienced with any tools before. Through their use these tools became extensions of her hands and spirit.

The same process began to occur with the tools of shop and garden. Though they had nearly all been purchased, our appreciation for them grew for other reasons. Many had been used for years by my grandfather and father, and had known their loving care. As we used these tools in the shop and around the ranch yard, we began to understand them in terms of the work they could do—the work they had so carefully been designed for through decades, even centuries, of trial and error and refinement. These were not simply expendable items, replaceable at the local hardware store. They had a history. They were part of our inheritance.

We took a new interest in the proper use and care of all our tools. We made racks and hangers for them so that each one had its proper place. We tried to develop a discipline about cleaning and returning them after use, and we found that this discipline did not come easily. We had far too long been conditioned by the built-in obsolescence and disposability so inherent in modern products.

Nevertheless, during the idle moments of winter, I worked over all the garden tools. I cleaned their metal parts and oiled them against the corrosive dampness of the coastal air. I sanded and oiled their handles, and in the process I learned more about their structure and design. I assembled a cartonful of old tools that had been abandoned in dusty corners, their handles broken, and took them with me to town one day to find replacement handles.

"You'd be far better off buying new ones," said the hardware clerk with a tone of authority in his voice.

"Perhaps," I ventured, "but I would hate to throw them away."

"Well, I guess they don't use the quality steel they used to," he conceded. "Those old ones will probably last you a lifetime. But this handle here will cost you almost as much as a whole new shovel."

"I'll take the handle," I replied.

As our sensitivity toward tools grew, we made another striking observation. Our tools became Pippin's most cherished toys. We have consistently forbidden cheap, breakable plastic items and frivolous toys. It has long been our contention that a large percentage of commercial toys are idle time-fillers that direct and prescribe a child's every move, precluding a real learning experience. Except for a fleet of substantial metal and wooden trains, trucks, and tractors, given by friends, and a set of wooden blocks that I cut from scrap—all of which he uses in a spirit of learning and creativity—Pippin plays most of all with our tools. Before the age of three he was helping eagerly with every construction project and knew the proper use for every tool, correcting us if there was one better suited for the task. We work side by side in the garden now, and if a shovel is too heavy for him, he uses a trowel. Our harvesting baskets and wheelbarrows are too big for him, so he uses a small basket and a little wagon instead. When he is not working with us, he plays with these items in a hundred real or fanciful ways. He respects them for the skills he has gained through their use, and he has retained the invaluable chance to be spontaneous and innovative.

Watching Pippin work with us around the house and on the land, we have gradually recognized another effect that our changing life-style has had upon our son. He both speaks and understands the vocabulary that emerges from nearly all our endeavors because, since we work at home, he is not isolated from them.

The children of our culture have become largely

separated from exposure to the working world of adults. It used to be that small towns and neighborhoods presented a rich blend of adult activities, which were accessible and largely understandable to young people. A child could drop by for a visit with the local grocer, blacksmith, banker, or postmaster. If he was not employed on the family farm or in the family business, he often held a job in the community where he had the opportunity to learn adult roles and skills. Increasing urbanization and industrialization, however, have dissolved family farms, driven local businesses from the community into huge conglomerate shopping centers, and concealed working adults behind the walls of distant factories and offices, where jobs increasingly complex and less comprehensible to children are carried out. Urban children today seldom witness, and even less often understand, what their parents do in the act of earning a living. This fact is one of the principal sources for the feeling of alienation that separates the young from the adult in our society.

Alienation only tends to be increased in the public schools, where classrooms are isolated from the larger community, often even from the school community itself. Students are asked to perform chores that do not prepare them for life in any way that is immediately apparent to them. A tremendous contrast exists between the attitude we have observed in children toward school and Pippin's attitude at home. When a fence needs mending, he is usually the first to see it and ask to help fix it because he has seen with his own eyes what goats or deer can do to a garden. When weeds begin choking the crops, he does not mind the work of pulling them because he sees us weeding and understands the need behind the chore. When tomatoes are ready to harvest, he helps because he, too, enjoys the salads and juice we make from them.

Pippin does not yet understand all that we do to earn a living, especially our creative work, in which he often cannot participate, but at the very least he is not deprived of the chance to observe us in the process. By witnessing and often joining in even the simplest adult work, he is learning about adult roles, developing a pattern of responsibility, and sharing in the satisfaction of making a tangible contribution to the common welfare.

As we have tried to teach ourselves new skills of basic living, we have become more and more aware of the gap that exists between us and the past. Before written language and even a long time after its invention, skills, traditions, and technologies were handed along verbally from generation to generation. Now spoken information and the system of apprenticeship have been replaced by the written word. We have found tremendous irony in the notion that while primitive peoples, without written language, were able to pass on their skills and their history through hundreds of generations, we, for all our printed verbiage, can scarcely transmit our heritage from one generation to the next.

Cultural change has so accelerated that the heritage of one generation is in many ways no longer relevant to the next. This in part accounts for our lack of continuity with the past. But at what point can we safely say that the past has nothing to teach us? Maggie and I have found in our own search frequent need to learn from the heritage of our ancestors and the native Americans who preceded them. There may come a time when this need is felt on a far wider scale.

Although our growing library of practical books was invaluable in some respects, we found them to be singularly unsatisfying. For a while we did not know why this was so, but gradually we became conscious that we missed the real teachers, the old-timers who knew their trades not from book learning but from long years of genuine experience. We searched our past for the skills we had learned from our parents and grandparents, and we found them easy to recognize. They were a part of us. I studied the encyclopedias of carpentry, but what I learned from my father firsthand stayed more firmly in my eyes and hands. Once in a while we checked a recipe book, but it was what we had observed directly that had the most permanent effect upon our cooking. We puzzled for hours over the mushroom books, trying to distinguish the edible ones from their numerous, confusing, poisonous cousins, but it was not until we finally found some old-timers with years of experience that we felt confident in picking a few varieties for the table.

Furthermore, while we found that there are hundreds of books filled with good advice about how to do this and when to do that, few of them had anything to say about how to find the spiritual energy to try. Whenever we learned from someone who loved his work and shared his wisdom, that spiritual energy was offered along with the facts. It came through in the twinkle of his eye or the tone of his voice. But for the most part, this we had to search for on our own, deep within ourselves. Far more than learning the skills themselves, this has been the hardest task.

Summers on our small farm are busy times. Long evenings are spent in the garden watering, staking or trellising vines, mulching, weeding, and harvesting. It is mostly during the early hours of morning, however, when fog hangs low over the lagoon and the kitchen is cool, that we do our annual fruit canning.

Since the damp coastal climate precludes large-scale drying of fruit, our winter stores must be preserved in jars. Canning fruit is not a new enterprise with us. Maggie learned it from me, I learned from my mother, and she from her mother. As far back as memory takes me, I have known the sweet summer smell of fruit boiling on the stove and the loud popping of lids as the jars seal.

The only fruit trees that remain around the ranch house are five gnarled apple trees, a winter pear, which blooms like a thundercloud in the spring, and three English walnut trees. Each fall, unless the squirrels discover them first, we shake about eighty pounds of walnuts and dry them in the house by the stove. We make full use of the apples and pears, but some fifteen other trees we have added to the orchard are still too young to bear. All the rest of the fruit is scrounged from our friends.

I learned long ago about the incredible amount of fruit that goes to waste across the land each year, particularly in towns. Surprisingly few people make use of the harvest they have right in their own yards. Maggie and I have for a number of years made the rounds each season picking fruit from the trees of friends or asking at the doors of people we have never met. I once even found a lady who paid me to pick her plums because she couldn't stand the mess they made on the walk!

Canning season begins with the cherry plums. They are followed by other plum varieties, peaches, apricots, pears, and finally apples. We have always made canning a joint venture. If friends or relatives visit on canning days, they, too, are put to work with knife and pot. By sharing the work and using the time for visiting and exchanging ideas, canning becomes not a solitary chore but a pleasant pastime. We do a bit at a time, and our satisfaction grows as the bounteous harvest accumulates and the pantry shelves fill.

We began in a small way, doing a few jars here and a little there as time allowed. Piece by piece our facility grew, and as we settled into a routine of increased efficiency, we gained more time to devote to winter stores. Maggie collected pickle recipes, and with cucumbers, cauliflowers, onions, green tomatoes, dill, garlic, cabbage, and other items picked from the garden, we added many kinds of pickles to the pantry shelves. Variety and quantity have grown so that now we put up about twenty different kinds of preserves each year, totaling between 350 and 400 quarts. To this we add numerous kinds of jams and jellies and the indispensable Italian pesto, made with parsley, sweet basil, garlic, and cheese blended together in a base of olive oil.

The most anticipated canning period comes with the fall apple harvest. We pick nearly a ton of apples from the old ranch yard trees early each October. Out comes the ancient cider press, and the sweet juices begin to flow. We hover around the spigot drinking glass after glass of the cold squeezings, and then we open the kitchen cannery in earnest. We put up applesauce and juice, setting some of the pressings aside for cider and wine. The house is draped with strings of apple rings so that we might also have a supply of dried apples on hand for winter munching. In the oven pies bubble and steam with autumn fragrance. These are happy times on the farm.

With the arrival of fall comes also the great squash harvest. Pippin and I look forward to this annual event anxiously as we explore among the vines during the summer months, inspecting the swelling, looming objects of green, yellow, orange, and pink. When the day finally comes, just before the first frost, the two of us start early in the morning with wagon and wheelbarrow. We make trip after trip to the house until the dining room is piled with over a thousand pounds and some three dozen varieties of gourds, pumpkins, and winter squash. Some are decorative, intended only for our autumn celebration of the pumpkin harvest. The rest remain on a long shelf in the dining room through the winter and are slowly transformed into soups, pumpkin bread, casseroles, and numerous baked dishes, serving in the meantime as a colorful feast for the eye and the soul.

Autumn for us is a mixed blessing, however, for it signals the time for slaughtering the goat kids.

The goat business began innocently enough. Before we moved to the Ranch, we saw Sunflower at the home of a friend and fell in love with her. She was just weaned, and we brought her home. She lived in the house with us, sleeping in the bathtub until I built a pen. In fact, Maggie slept in the bathroom with her the first couple of nights until she stopped crying for her former family.

When it came time to freshen her so that we would have milk, we found that bucks were scarce in the area. The first year went by, and she was not bred. Finally we obtained Snowballs; from that time on, we simply let proximity and the natural laws of procreation take their inevitable course.

Since the first offspring were both females, we were temporarily spared the full facts of goat-rearing. But by the time our second autumn rolled around at the Ranch, besides Amber we had Fig and Fog and Sienna's younger male kid. We knew that something would have to be done.

As the summer months waned, we judiciously avoided the subject. Apple harvest arrived and passed, with the squash harvest right on its heels. But gradually the unavoidable truth pressed itself upon us. We would either have to sell the little bucks to someone who would in turn kill them for the table, or we would have to slaughter them ourselves for our own use.

Both Maggie and I had eaten meat throughout our lives, but we had begun to question this part of our diet. As biologists we knew that pesticides and other poisons are concentrated along ascending levels of the food pyramid; we abandoned the consumption of the larger predatory ocean fish because of the questionable levels of mercury, DDT, and other chemicals they often contain. We were also concerned about the growing number of hormones and growth stimulants added to the feed of commercial beef and poultry, and the amounts of these meats that graced our table had become increasingly spare.

We were further disturbed by the impact of American meat consumption upon the agriculture of our nation and the diet of the world. Half the harvested agricultural land in the United States is planted to feed crops; 78 percent of our grain, not to mention soy beans and other high protein foods, is fed to animals. While beef provides protein of high quality, the production of that food is startlingly inefficient. A steer must consume twenty-one pounds of vegetable protein in order to yield one pound of meat protein for our use. Francis Moore Lappe, in *Diet for a Small Planet*, claims that the amount of protein fed to livestock and thus lost to human consumption is equivalent to 90 percent of the world's protein deficit.

These thoughts surfaced in conversation as autumn drew upon us. Another force also rose within us: since meat continued to be a part of our diet, we felt we should bear full responsibility for its consumption. Delegating the slaughter to someone else while we reaped the benefits began to appear as an evasion of knowing the full significance of eating meat.

We had performed the first half of animal husbandry. Through our auspices the does and the buck had come together in the production of these lives in order that Pippin might have milk. Maggie had learned to make yogurt, custards, and cheese from the extra, and our table had been rich with fine morsels. Mostly through our own efforts, the little goats had been fed, and we had learned from direct experience how much vegetable produce—how much land, sun, and water—a growing kid requires. These consequences we ourselves had perpetrated, save one still remaining, the taking of a life to sustain our own. This second and most difficult half of husbandry loomed before us like a dark cloud.

It is perplexing to me how the human mind copes with the act of killing. I spent years collecting insects, first as a hobby and later as a livelihood, and thought nothing of the countless tiny lives I snuffed out in the interest of science and self-education. Trout fishing in the Sierra was made only a trifle less enjoyable by the act of hitting the heads of live fish against a rock. Yet the more closely creatures share our lives or the more likeness they bear to our own attributes, the more difficulty we have in taking life from them.

Maggie and I knew these goats. We had raised them up from the miraculous moment of birth. The thought of killing them was emotionally abhorrent to us, though intellectually it was not. Yet, since childhood we had eaten beef, lamb, pork, chicken, and turkey without a thought of remorse for them and their brothers who had met their end in the well-hidden death chambers of the assembly line. For years we paid taxes to the government so that our armies could bomb and devastate a tiny country in Southeast Asia; we made our protests, but we paid our taxes just the same. And yet it was over three little goats less than half a year old that we shed our tears, because of all those ended lives for which we shared responsibility, it was these creatures alone that we had to look squarely in the eye.

We have a Bulgarian friend from the old country for whom every aspect of goat-raising comes as second nature. He had herded, bred, milked, and butchered goats since his early youth. We decided to ask him to help us with Fig and Fog so that we might learn directly from someone who had the complete confidence of long practice.

Boyan and his family came one Saturday morning. We tied a pair of hay hooks to a selected apple limb and brought out a tub for the entrails and a large pot for the organ meat. I sharpened a butcher knife of good steel and a skinning knife, and Boyan set to work in the matter-of-fact way of one who had learned the simple lessons of survival in a country far less removed from the facts of life than ours.

He selected Fig from the herd, hobbled his legs, and held him firmly over a small hole dug in the garden. With one deft stroke of the knife the act was done, quickly and without a whimper. In an instant the little goat's life ebbed away, and he lay limp upon the damp earth, his blood seeping slowly into the pit.

We hung the kid by his hind legs from the hooks in the apple tree, and Boyan showed Maggie the quickest, simplest way to dress him out. The skin was set aside for tanning, the head was neatly cleaned, the organs saved. He even showed us how to clean the small intestine by inverting it over a stick, for in Bulgaria this is prepared as a delicacy. Nothing is wasted.

When Fog had been similarly prepared, we hung the meat to cure, gave Boyan the heads to roast and some of the meat in exchange for his assistance, and bid the family farewell.

Soon the meat began to appear on our dinner table. There is hardly anything in this world more delicious than kid goat, and we had no compunction about eating it. But many weeks passed before I was able to face the fact that one little buck remained in the pen. Soon his meat would grow tough; his time, too, had finally come. I took the knife one morning and left the house alone.

For three million years or more our ancestors and other hominids from which they evolved had been hunters. From the long silent dens of *Australo-*

pithicus have emerged skull after skull of the animals upon which these ancient man-apes preyed, their cranial indentations and the bone weapons that fit them speaking of our heritage across the millennia. How thin is the veneer of civilization! How much thinner still are the plastic wrappers of roast and steak on the supermarket shelf, which in the last wink of time have sheltered almost an entire people from the realities of subsistence.

Our parents, and certainly their parents, had almost all known the facts of birth, death, and slaughter on the farm from firsthand experience. In one or two generations a break with the past had been created which now loomed before me like a dark and foreboding chasm. No amount of biological training concerning the natural laws of tooth and claw could fill this void. I had been told that life was sacred, even while the roast simmered in the oven. No one had taught me how to deal with the soft, frightened eyes that now looked up at me from beside the small pit I had dug in the ground.

I pulled the knife quickly through flesh and artery. The little goat flinched for an instant, then lay still. The centuries fled past before me. So this is our heritage, I thought. This is the same hand that paints a great canvas, builds a hydrogen bomb, and pens the dictum "Thou Shalt Not Kill."

I hung the little body from the tree and returned to the house.

"He's ready," I said to Maggie. "The next lesson is yours to learn."

She dressed the goat kid well. Another skin was set to tan, more meat was added to the larder, and that night we feasted on the head and organs as others had done uncountable times both before and after the dawn of civilization.

We had not assumed in haste this task of killing, but rather had waited until the time was right, until we were at least partially able to understand the significance of our actions. There had been no feeling of conquest, no thrill of the hunt, no sense of *machismo*, that peculiar flexing of one's manhood which may have played an important role in tribal life but which, in the modern hunter with his accurate scope and high-powered rifle, seems crude and out of place. We viewed the taking of a life as the gift of life, just as others had for centuries before us.

Since our first experience, we have grown more accustomed to these raw facts of life on the farm. Still, a gradual change has occurred. We have used less and less meat in our cooking. Many days pass, during which beans, cheese, grain, and eggs constitute our only protein. Maggie has developed a host of delectable dishes based upon dry soy beans or fresh favas. When we do use meat at all, it is in the style of the Chinese—as a sparing, flavorful garnish. A roast will last us a week, and one whole goat kid, less then twelve pounds of meat, will feed us for a month.

This change has not been the result of economics; except for a little extra feed we must purchase, our meat comes free. It is the act of raising the goats from birth that has influenced our thinking. We have begun to appreciate deeply that life is precious and must not be taken lightly. We now know how difficult it is to kill.

A spirit of moderation has gripped us in other areas besides the consumption of meat. As we have slipped into the routine of daily subsistence and have relocated most aspects of our livelihood to the home base, we have found that both the necessity and the urge to drive have vastly decreased. Shopping for staples has been reduced to a few market trips a year. To meet the more frequent needs, such as procuring eggs, butter, or occasional items used up in the kitchen, Maggie has re-instigated the nearly lost art of barter.

It would be hard to imagine walking into a supermarket with an armload of produce to trade for eggs, and, indeed, this she has not tried. But fortunately, numerous health food stores and small markets have sprung up in our region, and the keepers of these stores, particularly in the villages two miles away on either side of us, are more flexible in their approach to business. When we have extra produce in the garden, we pick the nicest items—cauliflowers, cabbages, gorgeous heads of purple kale, boxes of crisp romano beans—and while they are still garden fresh, Maggie makes a trip to the village. The joy she has discovered by engaging in this personal, adventuresome means of exchange and the friendly human contacts that have arisen in the process are commonplace experiences in nearly every country of the world except our own.

We are not entirely self-sufficient on our little farm at Audubon Canyon Ranch, nor can the local villages entirely meet our needs. Those purchases of goods and services that must be made in the larger towns are saved up until a full day's trip is justified, and every two or three weeks we make the run. Once we had ceased the usual humdrum daily confrontation with the urban world, it was astonishing how quickly we lost our defenses against it. Now a day of noise, smog, traffic, and crowds completely exhausts and disorients us, and when we are obliged to make a rare sojourn into San Francisco itself, nearly a week is required for full recovery.

We have also made a concerted effort to reduce our use of electricity since moving to the country. Before Audubon Canyon Ranch procured this place, the old house had been remodeled inside and completely rewired. An all-electric kitchen and electric heaters were installed. It cost seventy dollars a month to heat the house to accepted American standards in the winter.

The average home in this country contains twenty-one electric appliances. We took stock of those the house contained and the few we had brought with us, and counted nineteen in all. The Franklin stove from our former cabin was promptly installed, and the use of nearly all heaters discontinued. Living-room and dining-room lights were replaced with kerosene lamps, which we use selectively and sparingly, and the hot-water heater we turned to low. One day the dishwasher went up in smoke, and it has been used ever since as a cool place to store cheese. When the blender stopped working, we replaced it with a hand-cranked gristmill, which does nearly everything the blender could do and much more. When the toaster burnt out, we used the top of the Franklin stove instead.

Still, we have not tried to be purists about the use of electricity. Our fluorescent desk lamps are efficient sources of light and will stay. We have kept the refrigerator until we build a proper cooler, and the freezer will remain in use until we learn

another way to store meat. Maggie uses only cold water in the washer, and clothes are hung out on the line except during the worst weather.

Most of these changes could be made by anyone with little strain. Reducing our consumption of electricity has not made us any less comfortable, for we have simply adjusted accordingly. In fact, we can barely sleep in a thermostatically heated house now that we know the feeling of fresh air and cool nights. In one way, however, we are more fortunate than most. We live in a benign climate where winters are short, and the trees that fall each winter across roads or trails give us a steady supply of firewood. But to this must be added the fact that we have chosen to work for fuel; others have lived here before us who never used the wood even though it fell in abundance around them.

Cutting and splitting wood is one of the most satisfying of our numerous chores. Bit by bit during the summer months the job is done, and a little vigorous morning exercise puts me in order for the day. When the woodshed is full, we feel a sense of satisfaction that cannot compare with the monthly payment of fuel bills. And there is nothing in the world like stoking the stove on a cold morning or smelling the sweet aroma of burning wood while we sit by a crackling fire on a stormy winter evening. We have as a species enjoyed the warmth and glow of a fire too long to dismiss it lightly.

For years Maggie and I had talked of having a wood-burning cookstove. We finally found one in a local antique shop for a fair price and brought it back to the Ranch. There is no describing the joy this one material possession has added to our lives. The first pot we placed on the hot metal danced as if it were a symbol of the excitement we felt over a wood-cooked meal. The oven bakes our bread and many of our dinners. Cast-iron pans or kettles simmer on the back of the stove while yogurt is being made in the warming oven, and all this from the same energy that heats the living quarters. In the morning Pippin helps me fill the firebox, and together we hover around the old black stove rubbing our hands until the metal heats up. Soon breakfast is cooking, tea water is boiling, and toast is browning, while Bo sleeps in the warmest corner and Maggie and I warm our feet on the oven door, reading the morning paper in the old family rockers. We never experienced a comparable family gathering around our electric range.

Hemingway once said, "I have always believed that the man who has begun to live more seriously within begins to live more simply without." This we are finding to be true, but we are also convinced that the percentage of chance for the reverse to occur is very high as well. Learning basic skills, doing things by one's own efforts, knowing the origins of the substances we use and their final destination—the very acts of simple living seem to cause one to live more seriously within. One would have to be blind in the broadest sense to eliminate extraneous appliances and not see that energy is being saved; one would have to be profoundly insensitive to grow a few vegetables and not sense his connection with the essential processes of the natural world.

Our gradual return to a more basic way of life has slowed us down. Though our days are full and busy, our long-range pace has slackened, and the urgency we once felt about daily affairs has subsided. We now tend to measure growth and achievement in terms of years rather than days. As a result, each moment has grown richer, and each experience, no matter how small, more fulfilling.

We have learned during this three-year beginning that the simple life, particularly now in this time and place, is elusive and fraught with as many pitfalls as satisfactions. We have learned that the search can only be measured in terms of a lifetime, for it has taken us this long just to unfurl the sails and set our course.

Most important, however, seeking the simple life has drawn us together as a family. This has been our greatest reward.

3

FAMILY

We have come to love the seasons by the things we do together as a family.

When Pippin was still very small, he simply joined whatever mutual enterprise Maggie and I initiated. First in the backpack and later on foot, he accompanied our explorations. As his ability to walk increased, he took pride in leading on the trail. Short forays to gather chantrelles, which poke up orange and succulent from the leaf mold beneath our favorite live oak, or picking miner's lettuce as we walked up the canyon to clean leaves from the water-line screens became seasonal adventures to which we looked forward with great anticipation. Gradually our walks together increased in length. By the age of three Pippin was able to hike four miles at a time in rugged country without losing the spirit of joy and discovery.

Many of our family activities, particularly in the garden and around the ranch yard, have arisen out of necessity. They are routine chores made light in the sharing, and through them Pippin has developed a surprising level of responsibility and a number of skills. Many other things we do together, however, we have carried with us since our own childhood. Thus we found ourselves drawn

to the marsh one winter day for the purpose of bursting cattails.

Having picked several of the plump, dry seed heads, we pinched them one by one until the fuzz burst forth and took to the wind. Maggie and I marveled at this remarkable form of seed dispersal. Marshes are few and far between across the land, and cattail plants must have some way of reaching these widely scattered places, which constitute their only home. They have developed minute seeds, each one attached to a tiny plume and all of them packed by the uncountable thousands into the familiar "cat's tail." As the stalk dries, the seeds and their plumes are placed under pressure, and at some point during the winter the cattails explode, on their own if not helped a little by the jostling wind or fun-loving passersby like ourselves. Once liberated, the seeds are readily airborne and may be carried hundreds of miles on the wind. Those that fall on the water float in a thin film and may become stuck to the feet or feathers of waterfowl, which in turn distribute them to another pond along the flyway.

This interesting circumstance we had only learned about in recent years; it was the child in us that remembered the joy of watching the clouds of fuzz rising into the air, and it was this simple exhilaration, unfettered with matters of the intellect, that we witnessed in Pippin. He stood transfixed as the seeds began their journey, and as he grasped the technique of bursting the cattails himself, he continued until every last one had been done and he, Maggie, I, and the entire marsh were blanketed as though a fresh snow had fallen.

This and numerous other activities from our past we have shared with Pippin, and in time he has learned to share in return. We slept a few summer nights beneath the Great Buckeye before Pippin was two, but since then he has most often been the one to initiate the idea. We drink hot chocolate, talk quietly, or read a story together as the kerosene lamp casts its soft light on the gothic arches of the buckeye ceiling. With Bo curled up between us and Pippin's cat, Tigger, tucked warmly beside him in his sleeping bag, we listen to the owls and watch the night fog consume the stars. We love these nights, but it is Pippin above all who falls asleep with satisfaction, having contributed to the family unity.

So it is with other things around the farm. He will take his little basket and lead the way for the garden harvest or take us to the marsh ponds in search of newts or frogs. Frequently he asks us to join him in the "pueblo" he has built in our pile of potting soil or takes us beneath his giant bean tent where we sit together in the soft green light.

Freedom of spirit and spontaneity are the special gifts of childhood; willingness to listen and to follow the child's lead therefore become the principal responsibility and satisfaction of a parent. Children learn best by repetition, not so much of the things parents wish to teach them as of those that the children themselves want to learn. We have tried to listen to Pippin's callings, and in our doing so, learning has flowed both ways.

This process started most apparently as Pippin honed his ability with language. Maggie developed the technique of answering him by repeating what he said, not exactly word for word but by adding a word or a concept to it. At the same time that he heard his language and ideas verified, he also heard them extended and refined. So, too, when Pippin has asked us to join in building with his blocks, we have stretched his experience with balance and design a little bit at a time. During each requested visit to the marsh, we have gone one step beyond the familiar frogs and newts by observing something new about them or learning something else of interest along the way.

We have thus kept a constant challenge before Pippin as he has grown, not one we have imposed upon him but one that has evolved from whatever he himself has initiated. Our experiences together as a family have therefore been spontaneous and innovative. We have had no need for programmed activities or planned recreation. By simply following the lead of a child—and thereby also the child within ourselves—we have not hungered for adventure, because adventure has developed of its own accord.

Even the routine of daily living becomes an adventure when one approaches it as a child does.

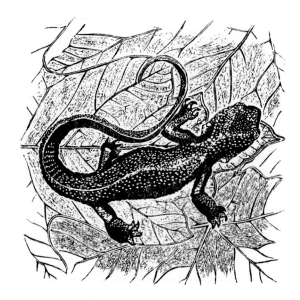

When Pippin and I walk to the mailbox each day, we never know what new discovery we may make in the process; when Maggie works with Pippin in the flower garden, they cannot predict what new use they may discover for a tool or what insight they may get about the way plants grow. Therein lies the sense of mystery, and we have discovered it anew by listening to Pippin and to the spirit he has kindled within us.

No matter how enjoyable one's occupation or way of life may be, daily living is fraught with less than stimulating chores. The often rigorous discipline necessary to sustain our small farm, earn a living, and raise a family has taught us that good habits are essential. They have rendered more efficient the carrying out of routine functions so that more time is available for creative pursuits, which require freedom of mind and spirit.

Habits of any kind can easily become self-limiting; their cultivation must be watched with vigilance and constant evaluation. But those that yield freedom of time and freedom of mind are necessary in developing the fine art of self-discovery and introspective living. Good habits should be a part of one's being. Of those we now have, some have remained with us since childhood, while others we are learning with great effort. It has been satisfying to see Pippin develop good work habits from the start, some automatically and some with only slight encouragement, as he has shared in the responsibilities of our daily affairs.

It has been equally satisfying to observe Pippin's growth, both physically and mentally, as a separate individual. One of his earliest expressions of independence occurred when he was just eighteen months of age. I had been photographing him for quite a while one day when, tired of tolerating my entreaties, he plucked a tomato from a pile ripening beside the window and stuffed it without hesitation into the lens of my camera! As he has participated in work and play around the Ranch, his proficiency has grown, and so also has his sense of independence and individuality. Therefore we also have not denied him the resulting development of self-confidence and self-expression.

The discipline required in our search for a basic, rewarding way of life has revealed much to Maggie and me about our own individuality as well. Assuming roles, trading roles, and dealing with life as a family have laid bare our basic natures as man and woman. We have come to understand that the male and female of our species have evolved differently. The child-rearing ability, as Norman Mailer has said, puts women closer than men to the mystery of life. Women tend to be subjective, intuitive, and sensitive to emotions because biologically they have had to be in order to carry out the act of motherhood. Throughout our evolution males more often have been hunters, providers, protectors, and custodians of tribal beliefs. Survival has demanded that they be objective, pragmatic, and intellectual.

These ancient biological differences find definite expression in Maggie and me. We have tried not to deny them even though because of them we often clash, for we have also discovered that the lack or imbalance each of us recognizes in himself creates a need that is partially fulfilled by the other.

This need for balance must be fulfilled internally as well, for in every man there is a little bit of woman, which also must not be denied; and in every woman there is a little bit of man. Perhaps the most difficult challenge in our relationship has been for us to bring out in each other that opposite side of ourselves, so that we might become more fully whole as human beings. It has been rewarding beyond compare that Maggie has begun to feel strong as a woman yet free to express and explore her conscious mind and intellect, while I have begun to feel fulfilled as a man yet free to experience my subconscious and express my emotions.

This process has required much effort, temperance, and understanding. As we have taken our steps together as a family, countless hours both agonizing and joyful have been spent evaluating subjectively as well as objectively our actions and our decisions. From the strength of our growing individuality has gradually emerged the strength of our unity.

Friends have often suggested that we have been able to accomplish much together because of common interests. Before the dawn of civilization, every man and woman who shared life together had by necessity at least one common interest, and that was survival itself. For most people in the world, this circumstance still prevails. Even in our culture, with all its comforts and ease, in times of crisis more couples have grown close together than have been torn apart, for survival as a family is an immensely powerful force. Rather than being forced into a position of sharing, however, we have chosen it. It is true that we began our relationship on the basis of common interests; the rest we have developed by simply listening sensitively to each other.

As we have sought to learn both the psychic and manual skills necessary to live as a family close to the land, we have encountered a gap between us and the past. Old-timers who could teach us directly have not been a frequent part of our experience. As a result, our search has led us back toward our own roots, and in the process of exploring our heritage, we have grown closer to our parents.

After leaving home, undergoing our own personal revolutions, and setting our course in life, we now find ourselves returning to the strengths of our parents, having also gained some perspective of their shortcomings. As children we were at the same time sensitive and blind to our parents'

various qualities; we can see them better now in retrospect. Quite often our way of life calls forth recollections of the values and skills we learned from them, and the recent times we have spent together have been enriched as a result of this discovery.

The experiences we cherished as children must have been guiding us in our life together all along, for as we have begun to give them voice, we recognize them as the very things we have chosen to incorporate in our attitudes and life-style.

In a physical sense, we have reached out for the objects that symbolize this heritage. We use big, cast-iron cooking pots and an old pancake griddle handed down through Maggie's family, rocking chairs, tools, handcrafted quilts and clothes over a century old that have come to us from my family, and numerous fruit-canning jars, the rims of which have been ground smooth by my grandfather from re-use over many years. Maggie's favorite clothes are those her mother made for her with infinite care and patience.

But the activities of daily living bear most the joy of memory. Maggie remembers the warm glow in the family fireplace, quiet times spent both together and separately, evenings of singing and homemade music, weekend picnics and camping trips in the country, and good times with the family pets. By the age of six she had learned to sew, and from her mother she learned also to knit, crochet, bake bread, and make good pies.

I remember that my father worked at home and was always there when I needed him. As a family we tended the garden, canned fruit, hiked and explored the hills together, and spent many quiet evenings listening to music. I remember long evening discussions around the dinner table, and a thousand images often float before me of my grandparents' old family homestead in the country where I spent summers—the orchard, the big kitchen with wood and coal-oil stoves, the chime of the big clock that now hangs on our wall, and the wild creek to explore nearby.

These things that meant most to us we have activated again. This heritage we could no longer quiet; it simply welled up from within. Nor have our parents forgotten entirely what they gave us during those years, and now we share with them in return as they join in family gatherings.

There is no question that some of our best family times together have revolved around the dinner table. Maggie and I both come from a long line of good cooks. Since earliest childhood, eating has meant more to us, however, than mere sustenance; it has represented a sharing of real craftsmanship and a time for coming together. In our families we knew none of the mealtime fragmentation that has become commonplace in our culture; the children always ate with the parents at the same table. Good food and good conversation went hand in hand and drew us together.

Our own adventures in the kitchen have brought

us closer to our family heritage. My family provides an interesting example of how roles and traditions can flex from one generation to the next. Grandma Mabel, on my mother's side, was typical of the age-old matriarchy of the kitchen. A superb if somewhat traditional cook from the Midwest, she nevertheless disliked much of the drudgery she made of preparing meals. Grandpa Dave grew an enormous vegetable garden, but his forays into the kitchen never exceeded the frying of bacon and eggs. When canning time came each year, he picked from the family orchard, and Grandma did all the rest.

My Italian grandmother, Nona, was also a traditional cook, but what a tradition! Roast duck, ravioli, tagliarini, torta, and dozens of other incredible dishes graced the family table. She worked long and hard over her productions without any help from Papa, but she loved it. Cooking for her was the special calling of motherhood.

Nona's brother, James Boitano, and his wife, Mary, lived with the Sanguinetti family on a spacious Mokelumne River farm in the Mother Lode country. Aunt Mary and Kate Sanguinetti were fabulous cooks. They were resourceful, for they had to work with whatever was at hand—vegetables and fruits in season, milk, eggs, and meat from the farm, occasional fish, deer, quail, or doves brought in by the men. It was a tough life, and division of labor was called for. The men were busy with the heavier chores and with their jobs in the mines. The women were left with the garden and the cooking.

My father, Milton, and his brother, Eddy, grew up in the city but spent summers on the farm. Most of Milt's love for the out-of-doors, which I felt as a child, had its origin in the wilds of the Mother Lode. From the women on the farm and their mother at home, Milt and Eddy learned to love good food, and at an early age they began to experiment with cooking.

My father and uncle are artists. Everything they have done over the years has been executed with

simmered fragrantly on the stove. As we scraped the little squares from the table, the spatula fairly sang, and its metallic ring became the music of this special event.

On Thanksgiving morning Maggie dressed and stuffed a duck, covered it with clay sculpted and decorated appropriately, and put it in the oven to bake. When the family assembled, we had a feast of many courses. The food was delicious, but more than that the family was bonded anew, three generations together at the same table sharing this little bit of history that had been restored.

craftsmanship and creativity. They began a new family tradition of spontaneous, creative cooking. And they broke the cycle of the kitchen matriarchy; from then on everyone cooked.

Holidays were special times in Maggie's family as well as mine. These were warm, happy gatherings, and the dinner table was always richly adorned. After Maggie and I moved to the Ranch, we decided it was time to share in return the festivities we had cherished as children, so we invited our parents for Thanksgiving. My uncle had passed along to us Nona's ravioli recipe, a special dish that had been in the family for over a century. Two days in advance we began preparations.

On a big worktable we rolled the dough until it was nearly thin enough to see through. Though we knew from the recipe what ingredients to use for the filling and the sauce, the particular skill of making ravioli we had to learn ourselves. The first batch we stuffed too full. When we pressed the folded dough with the ravioli roller, many of the little pockets burst, and we had to seal each one with a fork.

Eventually we caught the technique and rolled and cut ravioli by the hundreds, while the sauce

It has always been that some members of a tribe live far beyond the age of procreation and child-rearing. Why should this be so? Of what advantage are old people to the basic cause of survival?

This turn of human evolution must have something to do with culture—the transmission of the mysteries, laws, values, and skills that together constitute cultural heritage. It must be no accident that the oldest members of tribal societies were always looked upon as the wise men, or that the religious sages of the Sioux Indians were the six sacred grandfathers. It is tragic that the pace of change in our culture has left the aged behind without a role in society, often without even so much as a home.

My father came to live with us for a time while my mother was away. We worked together on a hundred different projects; he spent hours of each day with Pippin, and he shared in our various joys and difficulties. We realize now from his contributions to family unity how alone we have been as a small, nuclear family. The jobs he did were jobs we therefore did not have to do. The wisdom he shared was wisdom we did not have. And his role with Pippin was a role we ourselves could not fill.

There is much to be said for the value of an

extended family. The spread of age and experience, and the availability of many hands to carry out the act of daily living seem all the more important to us since we have begun to live closer to the land. On a farm, where there are roles for everyone to fill, the extended family once prevailed. In learning to work again with our parents, we are restoring this tradition in our own lives.

We have also discovered that a family is larger even than the extensions of actual family relationship. Over the years Maggie and I have been drawn close to people older than ourselves who have become in a very real sense spiritual parents, and we in turn have become a spiritual family for young people who have come to live with us for weeks or months at a time. These relationships are deep, as permanent as any hereditary relationships can be, and from them we have gained much satisfaction.

Whatever the nature of our experience as a family and whatever the definition of family bounds, we know this to be true: the things we do together today, tomorrow become Pippin's heritage. Who knows what experiences, what values, what skills he will remember as he faces his own future? The richness of experience he gains from us now will be his most important source of strength later on. Raising a child is more than providing food and shelter and clothing. It is an act of family responsibility and an act of family love.

Teaching and Learning

Exploring the natural world and working in the garden together have been profound experiences. In growing up close to the land, Pippin began learning about the plants, animals, and essential processes that exist around him even before he knew the words to describe them. For all of us the thrill of discovery that pervades our daily affairs has been like scaling an unclimbed peak or charting an unknown sea.

One of the responsibilities we accepted in moving to Audubon Canyon Ranch was to develop an educational program in which students could live and study in a natural setting. Through this experience, our need to share with others what we love and what we are learning has found its most rewarding expression.

A dragonfly emerging from the pond, a pacific giant salamander prowling along the stream, and a ctenuchid moth caterpillar feeding in the marsh are part of the daily vocabulary of a student's stay in the canyon.

Sometimes the students witness the power of natural forces at work upon the land. Delicate earthworm tracery and wave ripples on the mud after a violent winter storm are gentle decorations that cannot hide the fact that a bit of the watershed has been moved toward the sea.

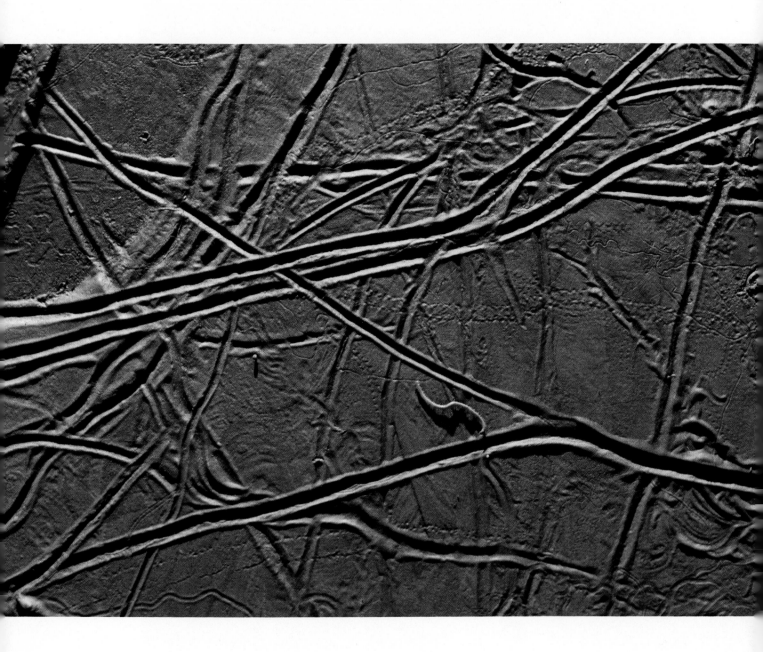

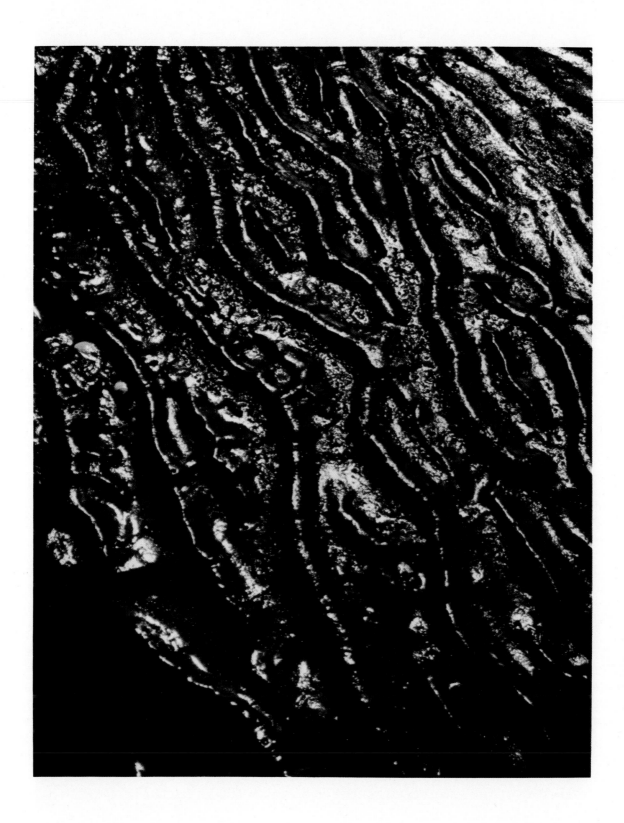

At other times we experience together the growth surge of spring—leaves reach for the sun, flowers burst from their buds, and even the deepest scars of winter are healed.

Though we set out to teach biology and ecology, we discovered that the very way in which we live offers meaning for others who share the canyon with us, for learning manual skills also expands one's understanding of self and the larger world. Spinning and dying wool, baking bread, and cooking meals together are simple events that bring us closer to a basic philosophy of life.

We supplement our meals with native foods gathered from the wilds
around us. A basket filled with mushrooms picked from beneath the
ancient oaks, and the earthy aroma of their cooking, speak to us of the
native Americans who once camped beneath these trees and of the
foraging heritage that is common to all mankind.

Visiting students harvest as much of their food as the garden will supply. Inside the fence as well as outside, they learn that they must contend with myriad other hungry creatures that seek the same tasty members of the plant kingdom as they—the delicate white butterflies whose larvae ravage Chinese cabbage, the sparrows that make lace of squash leaves during autumn migration, and many other species both native and introduced.

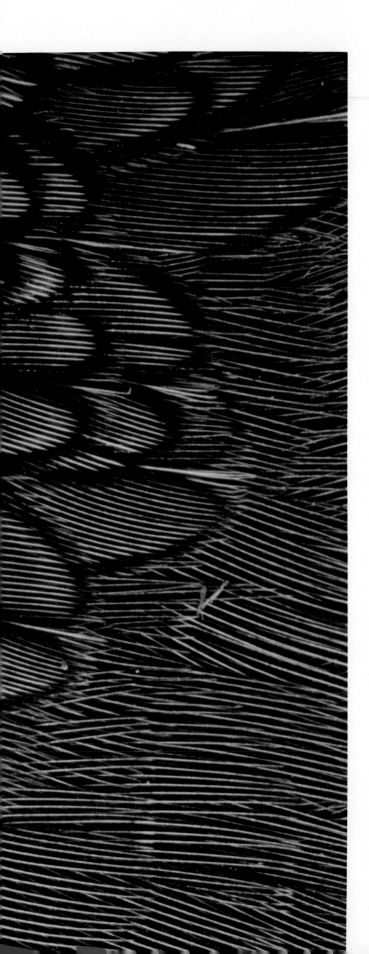

Within the garden we view the quail as a threat to our sustenance; beyond the fence the quail becomes a masterpiece of behavior and design, a constant companion, an important element in the food webs of other species. We do not hide this duality of feeling, for the same students who help chase the quail from the garden may another day see a Cooper's hawk strafe the flock in pursuit of its own sustenance.

One year a massive migration of California tortoiseshell butterflies invaded the region and settled. They laid so many eggs that the resulting larvae completely stripped their food plants of leaves. When the next generation of adults emerged, the canyon was carpeted with butterflies sipping moisture from the streambanks. The rise and fall of the tortoiseshells was a stark lesson in population dynamics.

For us the beauty of teaching has been discovering a feeling of mutual apprenticeship. In teaching as in rearing children, the teacher stands to gain as much from the students as they in turn gain. By choosing to live close to an urban center, we have received from students and friends alike the intellectual stimulation that the ferment of urban life provides, while sharing in return what knowledge, skills, and peace of mind we have gained from living close to the land.

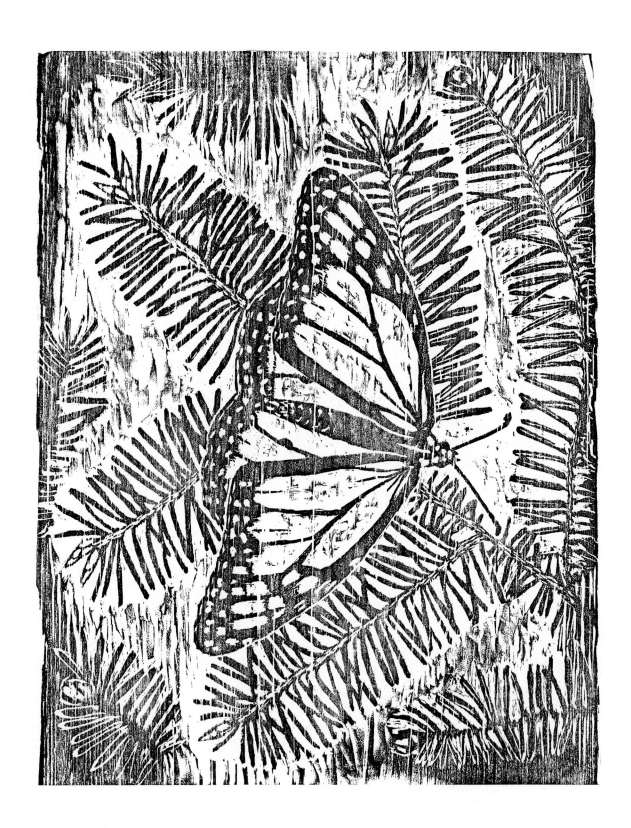

4

SHARING

When he was in the seventh grade, Craig Curley came to the canyon to spend his first day as a student with us. He walked quietly down to the marsh and lagoon shore, exploring, feeling, getting a sense of the land and its many inhabitants. When he returned home, he wrote a theme for his English class that began with these words:

"Audubon Canyon Ranch is a small, beautiful place with redwoods towering above the lagoon, shorebirds skimming across the gray-blue water, and wisps of mist rising from the water and between the trees. The ranch house looks like a mansion nestled in a field with beautiful light green grass, with a babbling stream running near. In the morning the sounds are unique. The creek gurgles, blackbirds sing, herons and egrets clack in the background, but very near you hear the sound of the quail in the scrub calling 'chi-ca-go,' drawn out, and their staccato 'bleep-bleep-bleep.'"

Michele Heydel came to the Ranch with her sixth-grade class and later wrote about a hike with two friends to the canyon fern grottos. "We walked up through the forest . . . going higher up to where plants like those in the dinosaur age grew, sipping the cool, fresh stream water and

resting every so often, picking up and exploring everything new by just lifting rocks, but also returning everything. I could have stayed there forever and never realized there was another world, a world that is becoming more and more ugly by the touch of man."

These are the impressions of youth. They were not formed from the pages of a biology book; they emerged instead from actual experience. Book learning is a vital supplement to nearly every educational process, but the most substantial learning happens as a result of the doing itself. This suspicion we already had when we came to the Ranch; the students, however, and particularly Pippin as he has grown, have convinced us that it is actually so.

Maggie and I both strongly rebelled against our college training, for in all but a few university experiences, we found that the actual rowing was reserved for the graduate oarsmen. Most college education—and, for that matter, the long years of training that are directed primarily toward it— seemed to us to be based on the premise that only when one has mastered a fund of knowledge should one be allowed to put that knowledge to the test of actual practice. The natural pyramid of the learning process seemed to have been turned upside down.

Had my parents prevented my participation in gardening until I knew as much about the subject as they did, I might never have begun. Since gratification was not deferred, however, my interest in cultivating plants grew and flourished at its own natural pace. Fortunately, not all of our formal education was devoid of this kind of direct experience. We both had some excellent teachers along the way, without whose direction and inspiration our interests might not have maintained their momentum. Maggie recalls in particular a bit of field work in biology that completely changed the direction of her life.

Learning by experience and discovery has been the main premise of our teaching at the Ranch from the beginning. For three years we have experimented, working with varied combinations of ages, trying different lengths and sequences of learning programs, testing new avenues of study, but always exploring together with those who come to share the canyon with us. We have learned something about how the students respond to the canyon, about their needs for work space and tools, and about optimum numbers of participants. Most important, we have achieved a greater understanding of the learning process. We believe above all that discovery and sharing are the seeds of learning.

During the first year we established the research associate program of Audubon Canyon Ranch. The original nucleus of associates has grown to include a blend of junior high, high school, and college students as well as adults from the community, who spend one day a week at the Ranch throughout the school year pursuing their own natural history investigations. The program follows the principle of self-education more than that of refined research, since our concern is more the learning process than the end result of the studies. It is a beginning place for those who have a keen interest in the natural world, a springboard from which the

students can move in the direction of either teaching, or more sophisticated scientific study, or in any event a lifetime of fascination with the world we inhabit.

Some of the students, both old and young, have a rich biological background. Some studied natural sciences many years ago and struggle now against minds grown rusty through too long a time divorced from exploration and investigation; others have only recently come upon the mysteries of biology. Regardless of background, we all experience the joy of discovery, the excitement of learning, and a collective good humor as we plod through field and marsh in old clothes and boots.

Two of the associates have begun a long-range plant-succession and bird-population study on a south-facing slope of the canyon that has been slow in recovering from logging many decades ago. As woodland and forest trees gradually reclaim their former territory from the coastal scrub, the birdlife that frequents the slope will undoubtedly change. The associates' particular interest is establishing a process by which visiting students can document this transformation over a period of many years.

Another group began an investigation of the marsh ponds shortly after they were dug. Besides learning about the breeding behavior of newts and two species of frogs, and the succession of marsh plants that invaded the open water, they discovered from direct observation the reason why we never suffer from mosquitos in our canyon.

Two days after the ponds were created, the surface of the water was dotted with hundreds of mosquito egg rafts. During the next weeks, however, the associates chronicled the decline in the number of mosquitos, adult and larvae alike, as the swallows arrived and dragonfly nymphs and other aquatic predators began to colonize the ponds. By late summer the canyon was filled with thousands of dragonflies, darting about after flying insects, assuming the role of aerial predators after the swallows had left on their long flight south. We never again witnessed a population explosion of mosquito larvae; the natural balance in the new ponds had been achieved.

Besides recording information relating to their own studies, the research associates have frequently entered miscellaneous observations in the natural history journals. They found a great deal to enter one day when, after the great storms of our second winter, they came to the canyon to continue their investigations.

The first storm had hit the coast like a hurricane. All night the rain poured down and the storm winds howled. Several trees fell in the canyon forest, and I still recall venturing forth the next day to saw wood. The rain had temporarily stopped, but the gale continued. Huge bay trees arched over me, flailing violently as though the world were approaching its final moment. I was engulfed by a deafening roar. Leaves and lichen and sticks were driven through the air like sleet in a blizzard; across the stream a big bay snapped with the sound of a rifle shot and crashed to the ground. I retreated from the forest in haste, almost in terror, like a timid creature out of its element. I looked back once toward this wild scene beset by turbulence, and I saw four vultures careening above the trees, tossed upon the swirling mist like ships on the sea. They were obviously having a splendid time! This monstrous assault from the Pacific was apparently the better part of their world.

No sooner had this storm moved inland than another replaced it, and directly on the heels of that one came a third. The rain never ceased all night, and the sound of it pounding on the roof made our sleep fitful. At dawn I went outside to survey the situation and found the canyon in a state of pandemonium. The stream had swollen beyond its banks; the marsh and drive lay deep

beneath the silt-laden flood. Severe winds and one of the highest tides of the year had driven the lagoon, too, over its customary shoreline, and every low piece of land was inundated.

As the rain subsided, we put Pippin in the backpack and went exploring into the canyon. Eleven inches of rain had fallen in the space of one week, and the downpour of the previous night had been the undoing of the precipitous canyon. Several mudslides had ripped down the steep canyon walls, carrying with them ferns, trees, and boulders. In some places trees had fallen into the stream, diverting its flow and causing tremendous erosion of its banks. The stream itself was a raging cataract of muddy water, and the roar of rocks rumbling along the bottom of the channel was deafening. Enormous tributaries had developed in every tiny side gully, even where we had never seen water flow before.

We fought our way along the crumbling banks of the canyon torrent toward our water system. We found the pipe at last, deeply buried beneath heaps of giant rocks. The forces were in action that gave this deep gorge its character. Grain by grain, stone by stone, the mountainside was yielding. The tiny work of man, this single pipe in a streambed, seemed frail and tenuous, caught in the powerful grip of erosion. Several days passed before a neighbor and I were able to dig the water system free. Meanwhile, we had a muddy supply from the storage tank.

That night the storm diminished and the flood subsided. The next morning we ventured down to the lagoon. The soft silt was richly decorated with the tracks of night animals—earthworms, beetles, foxes, and raccoons, which had come out in force in search of tidbits exposed by the flood. The lagoon shore was littered with debris. Sticks, logs, twisted roots of redwoods, and scoured rhizomes of canyon araleas were strewn about everywhere. New bars of mud and sand had appeared on the mud flats, and the delta of our stream had expanded noticeably. While the hillsides had lost a bit of their substance, the mud flats had gained accordingly. The salt marshes had a little more land to colonize. In one night the ephemeral lagoon had moved one small step closer to its eventual demise.

When the research associates came that morning, they hardly recognized the canyon. They found their study areas drastically changed. It was a stark lesson in the power of natural forces, and the associates stood in awe of them, even as we had during the height of the storms.

The most remarkable events recorded in the journals took place on Mouse Hill. Between our canyon and the rookery there is a grassy ridge, which for many years had been disturbed by grazing and harvesting of oat hay. When the dairy ranches became a sanctuary, the ridge was left to its own devices. The deeper soil of the fields quickly became infested with wild oats and introduced thistles, while the steeper, more rocky slopes gradually returned to native bunch grasses and coastal scrub.

The winter before our arrival at the Ranch had been a wet one. Late rains had pushed the oats and thistles to record heights. The next winter brought no storms to flatten the old stalks. As we walked over the slopes with the associates, little voles, normally secretive and mostly nocturnal, darted for cover everywhere ahead of us. The dry grass was riddled with their runs, and the crisp air thick with their rustling.

We learned that, provided with ample food from the season before and extra protection from predators beneath the stands of dry stalks, the voles had experienced an astonishing population explosion. They had fed upon the seeds and eaten every new blade of grass within these protected places, and now they were venturing into more open surroundings, clipping the grasses right down to their roots. Yet on the slopes above, where native plants had

returned over the years, the mouse population remained in a more balanced state.

As the dry summer approached, the voles became frantic with hunger, ravaging what little grass remained around the fringes of the fields. Then one of our students made a significant discovery: on a slope above a little ravine he found a large system of badger burrows from which great piles of dirt had been freshly excavated.

That evening we went quietly onto the ridge and settled down behind a small bush. We waited in silence until we were stiff from the tension of anticipation, and then suddenly, as the last rays of the setting sun crept up the slope towards the burrows, a badger poked its striped head above ground, tested the air for danger, and finally drew itself clear of the hole, followed within moments by its mate. None of us had ever seen a badger before. We crouched in wonder and delight behind our bush, hardly breathing as the badgers romped and played together. As darkness gripped the slopes, they struck off in search of voles.

During the summer, as the arms of the scale shifted, the boom and bust economy of a disturbed, unbalanced ecosystem became starkly apparent. Foxes and bobcats moved into the fields in such numbers that the grassland became webbed with their trails. Our pair of great horned owls hunted there each night, joined by owls from other canyons. Red-tailed hawks, kestrels, and white-tailed kites arrived in large numbers to share the bounty. And the badgers scoured the grassland until the ridge looked like a crater-pocked battlefield, for this was the effect of their powerful claws upon the land.

By the end of the summer the fields were silent. Not a mouse stirred. The hawks drifted away, and the badgers abandoned their home. Shrouded in summer fog, Mouse Hill became an eerie ghost of its former self, brown, desolate, and scarred.

When the rains returned in the fall, the fields became almost instantly green, but not with grass. Where oats had once been the dominant cover,

now only thistles grew. The torrential rains that tore the canyon asunder that winter saturated the fields until water poured from rodent burrows in spouting streams. Many gophers and some of the few remaining voles lay drowned and stiff upon the ground. The following spring, Mouse Hill became an impenetrable thicket of thistles, but this time few rodents remained to enjoy the protection of their cover. The predators did not return. The resident red-tail hawks and great horned owls were absent for long periods, hunting higher up on the ridge or other places where food could be found. The badgers disappeared entirely. A student finally found them again high up on the ridge near the edge of the forest.

It had been an incredible lesson in the effects of man and his weedy companions upon the population dynamics of wild creatures, and for all of us it had been a study in the importance of keeping a journal. By recording every observation, we had developed an accurate picture of the timing of events as the two contrasting seasons unfolded before us.

During the second year another event took place in the canyon which demonstrated population dynamics at work, this time quite apart from human intervention. In the middle of March a large migration of California tortoiseshell butterflies invaded our county. These butterflies normally breed inland and farther north in the state, and are rarely seen in our region. Perhaps overpopulated and pressed for food in their breeding grounds, they started moving southward, entering our area in droves, their wings tattered and worn from their long journey. Only once, many years before, when as a child I was beginning my first collection of insects, had I witnessed a similar migration.

One day late in April, I was hiking far up the ridge in the chaparral and discovered clusters of young tortoiseshell caterpillars on ceanothus, the wild lilac or blue-blossom shrubs. By the middle of May almost every ceanothus in the county had been defoliated. Great brown patches on the hillsides marked the leafless bushes where the ravaging hordes had been ruthlessly at work. The hungry larvae were soon on the move, crossing the local roads by the millions until their smashed bodies made the pavement slippery and hazardous for driving. Soon the caterpillars had pupated; so dense were the chrysalids on some bushes that they rustled like dry leaves as they gyrated in unison, loudly responding to the slightest disturbance.

At ten o'clock on the morning of June 11, as though every leaf of every tree had taken flight, the canyon was suddenly filled with butterflies. They swarmed in the warm summer breeze, their fresh new wings radiant in the sunlight. Later in the day, as the temperature rose, they flocked to the garden to drink from the damp earth and flew deep into the canyon, where they gathered on the wet stream banks more thickly than leaves on the forest floor.

The research associates observed these events, too, discussed them with us, and compared them with what we had learned on Mouse Hill. What would become of our new population of butterflies? Their food plants were bare, stripped by the hungry billions of caterpillars from which they had come. These were the ceanothus leaves transformed, these orange-and-brown creatures of the sky. Where would they lay their eggs? What would sustain the next generation? The bushes would push forth a new crop of leaves in the spring, but for how long could they sustain the chewing hordes? Surely the tortoiseshell population would dwindle just as the vole population did. Parasites, predators, disease, and starvation would swing the pendulum of numbers for a while in the other direction.

Maggie and I looked back upon the many family walks we had taken in the canyon and the observations that students and research associates had shared with us. We were beginning to realize that these experiences were prompting the very growth of our understanding. Living and working close to the land were allowing us time to experience the natural world, the peace needed to think about the relationships we were discovering, and the introspection necessary for their evaluation. The nat-

ural world, we were finding, is more than a pleasant environment in which to live. It is also a teacher of the highest order.

Our idea in beginning the research associate program was that students of natural history would be able to assist us in working with school groups in residence at the Ranch. We hoped that our own natural history investigations and the studies conducted by the research associates would become an evolving but continuous enterprise, and we suspected also that visiting children would gain far more from participating in a long-range process than they would from a program created solely for their benefit during their visit. This assumption has proven correct.

The associates have helped both by creating teaching and reference materials and by participating side by side with us in the teaching itself. The most exciting result of working together in a group has been the highly varied talents that have emerged. One lady, for instance, joined the program with no background in the natural world; she had worked as a graphic artist in fashion design, an experience that proved to be of the utmost importance in her studies at the Ranch. She began an investigation of the algae, protozoans, crustaceans, and insects in the ponds and stream; it lasted two years, during which time she assembled a remarkable fund of knowledge and created a collection of extraordinary drawings, which will benefit other students at the Ranch for years to come.

Another woman, also without previous natural history experience, quickly revealed a facility for meticulous work with her hands. She became enamored with bones and applied her unique manual dexterity to the task of cleaning and assembling skulls and skeletons. Her graveyard of animals found dead of natural causes has attracted much interest, particularly among the younger associates, and several students have joined her in what she calls "the fine art of skullduggery." As a result of their work, the Ranch is acquiring an excellent set of teaching materials, which reveal much valuable information about feeding adaptations and other aspects of comparative anatomy, not to mention the succession of organisms responsible for reducing a corpse to a skeleton.

When we have had groups of fifteen or so junior high and high school kids living with us at the Ranch for a week at a time, the research associates have come to continue their work with the students. They are not experts, and perhaps this is the source of their effectiveness. Like the visiting students, they are themselves in the throes of learning. With Pippin often in the lead, we all dive in together and continue the bird surveys, the marsh pond studies, behavioral observations, or the assembly of skeletons. As one girl said, "It's a very good feeling when you finally get the bones connected."

More often than not, we learn as much from the students as they do from us. If you assume you can learn from another person, there exists a ready basis for communication. This assumption lies at the heart of good teaching, and it applies as well to raising children. Learning flows both ways, as freely from student to teacher or child to parent as the reverse, as long as the peculiar ego and authority needs of the adult are not allowed to obstruct the learning process.

Maggie and I will always remember the first of several days we spent with one particular group of kids. It was a mixed group of nine sixth-, seventh-, and eighth-graders, most of whom had not known each other previously but many of whom had been keenly aware of their natural environment since earliest childhood. One girl, a natural leader, had become knowledgeable about birds and facile at finding their nests. The students arrived at nine-thirty in the morning and before lunch had established their camping spots, cut two days' supply of firewood, become thoroughly ac-

quainted with the goats, logged forty birds' nests on the ranch house and outbuildings, and located five redwing blackbird nests in the marsh. In one of these nests they observed a gopher snake eating the last two eggs, and in another they found a snake stealing one of the chicks—events we had not managed to observe in two years of residency at the Ranch! They also discovered five Brewer's blackbird nests in the apple trees and found several clusters of arboreal salamanders in the hollow limbs, all located only a few yards from the house. They found the violet-green swallow nest in one of the apple limbs, discovered an infestation of mealy bugs in the bark, and even observed microscopic wasps in the act of parasitizing them.

By the end of the day they had located no less than eighty bird nests in the canyon and, for a study of territoriality, had color-marked a large group of fence lizards by catching them with nooses made on the spot from stripped stalks of wild oats, a technique I had not once observed during ten years of associations with herpetologists.

All this they did on their own volition and by means of their own system of leadership and organization. By the time some of the research associates arrived the next day to share their knowledge with the students, the kids were quite prepared to teach them a thing or two, and the associates spent a day following them around, wide-eyed with wonder and admiration. If we learned anything during those few days, it was this: never underestimate the knowledge, skill, and potential of children.

Even so, the students had an important lesson in store, too: that error as well as success lies at the heart of learning. On the second day, when they took the research associates around to see the bird nests they had discovered, they found that many of those located near the ground were empty. Both eggs and young had vanished, and the parents had abandoned the nests. In the excitement of the first day's discovery, they had inadvertently trampled paths through the vegetation, which during the night some wily predators had followed. The anonymity of the sites so carefully chosen by the parent birds had been disturbed just enough by the eager students to give the predators access.

The children were crestfallen; the unexpected consequences of their enthusiasm took the wind clear out of their sails. In an effort to save those nests that had escaped the nocturnal marauders, they took rakes from the garden shed and pulled the flattened grasses and rushes upright again. From then on they proceeded across the land with a very light and cautious step.

We have continuously emphasized in our teaching that because so much remains to be learned in every branch of the natural sciences, a new and important discovery might at any moment be made. I know this from personal experience, for as a student I collected dozens of insect species new to science, some in seldom studied regions but others right close to home. An amateur insect collector in our own county discovered several new species of

harvestmen right in the hills of his community. Several local bird watchers recently made the rare observation of snowy owls in our area. One winter morning on the way to the mailbox I came upon a dead shrew on the driveway. When I looked at it closely I saw two tiny, pale beetles crawling through its fur like fleas, and I saved both the insects and the shrew for the California Academy of Sciences. The report came back that I had found two nest beetles, which are exceedingly rare in collections and about which very little is known.

The thrill of making a rare or entirely new discovery is unsurpassed. The adventure of science is equal to that of geographic exploration, the possibility for which has somewhat dwindled as man has come to know more completely the physical landscape. But the history of man's explorations repeats itself in each individual. For Pippin, each new clump of bushes is another world discovered; the first grasshopper he found might as well as have been the first grasshopper ever seen by man. We have observed the same sense of wonder in each of our students, and the distinct possibility that a discovery might be new not only to the student but also to the accumulated knowledge of man adds further excitement and anticipation to each investigation.

In our first class of sixth-graders there was a boy named Eric who had not quite caught the spirit of the canyon. He was somewhat obstreperous and, being a talented leader, had gathered several other boys into his mischievous ranks. On one visit to the Ranch he found a peculiar, sluglike grub at the edge of the drive and stopped to take a closer look. "Then it started to move," he later wrote, "so I got a leaf and picked it up. I brought it to Maggie, who immediately got excited and was complimenting me. I thought it was nothing, but Maggie made me feel like I rediscovered America. When we got together at lunch David explained the importance of this animal. He told me that this larva was a bot fly and that it is very rare to find this species and that they would take it to the University of California with my name on it. I felt very good about finding that bot fly."

From that moment on Eric was a devoted leader of the expedition.

Unlike the great discoverers of bird nests, who took the canyon quickly in stride, most children who study with us at the Ranch have had little exposure to the natural world. They are products of a high-pressure urban culture in which materialism has been their most influential yardstick for measuring the world around them, and when they arrive at the Ranch, they are running like noisy trains on a high-speed track.

At first, our relatively quiet way of life and the tranquillity of the setting are difficult for them to grasp. Sometimes it takes two or three days for them to "decompress"; but gradually peace and solitude have their effect, and the students begin to discover inner resources they often did not know they possessed.

It has come as a surprise to us that experiencing our way of life is almost of greater significance to the students than studying biology and ecology. One of the first events of a week spent with us is the baking of bread. On a big table outdoors many bowls are assembled. Working without recipes, the students learn from Maggie about the basic ingredients and begin with these. From then on, they add a variety of nuts, fruits, and grains of their own choosing, and before long the whole scene is richly plastered with sticky dough and flour of various colors. Sometimes Maggie also works with the students in making fire-baked eating utensils out of clay dug from the local hills, and at a glance I am often not sure which of these processes is actually taking place; but eventually a number of decent loaves emerge from the pandemonium and are left to rise in the sun before being

baked in the big beehive bread oven. We are one happy lot indeed when the hot loaves finally emerge, ready for sampling.

The students harvest some of their food from the garden and in the process learn something of the joy we experience in growing our own fruits and vegetables. They all share in milking the goats and making cheese, too, and occasionally they are lucky enough to witness the birth of goat kids. Once this great event has been enjoyed, the question ultimately arises: what will become of them all? The concept of killing must be faced, and as they dry the beautiful newborn kids with towels, they ponder this fact of life, each in his own way. It is a hard lesson that always reminds us of the void we ourselves had to span.

As they work with us in the garden, the students ask many questions about how we control insect pests and other marauders. They learn from direct observation the differences between the reasonably balanced populations that exist in the wilds beyond the fence and the unbalanced populations created by cultivation within. Killing must be faced again, for they see that an excessive population of snails, slugs, or rodents, once created by man, becomes his responsibility and must somehow be kept in check if the particular food web of which we are a part is to be sustained.

As a means of comparing our food web in the garden with that of a natural ecosystem, we like to visit the rookery with the students. We watch the parent birds as they return to the nests and feed their young. Then we walk to the shore of the lagoon so that we may explore the place from which the birds take their food. It is an amazing world that we find there.

In the muds and channels of this inland arm of the Pacific an intricate and splendidly balanced web of life exists, as vast and productive as any living system on earth. Like all other animals, including man, the herons, egrets, and other birds that feed in the lagoon are ultimately dependent upon plants for their survival. On the surface of the mud flats and in the tidal water that fills the lagoon twice a day thrive billions upon billions of diatoms, tiny one-celled plants capable, like all green things, of manufacturing food with the aid of sunlight. Sea lettuce and other algae at times nearly cover the mud at low tide. These plants are consumed, alive or as they decompose, by a multitude of small animals.

In addition to the algae, there are three plants of the salt marshes that produce a vast amount of food. Cord grass, which grows in deeper water along the outer margins of the marshlands, is known to be seven to ten times more productive than wheat, acre for acre, because when it decomposes during the winter, its entire substance becomes extremely rich food for scavengers such as amphipods and worms, and filter feeders such as clams and mussels. The pickleweed and salt grass that form the higher zones of marsh vegetation produce their share of food, too, and some decaying vegetation is washed into the lagoon by streams of the surrounding watershed.

We walk out onto the mud flats together. What seems from a distance to be a soggy wasteland proves to be one of the richest habitats for animal life on the face of the earth. As we probe in the mud and beneath the mats of sea lettuce, we find staggering concentrations of ghost shrimp, clams, mussels, amphipods, isopods, and many kinds of worms. These drab tidal expanses are a seething mass of life!

The small animals thus sustained by plant life in the lagoon form an immense food web, which supports some twenty-six kinds of fish, many of them the young of ocean species that depend upon lagoons and estuaries as nursery grounds. It is primarily upon these fish that the herons and egrets feed. Their sharp beaks and long legs superbly designed for spearing and wading, they hunt along the deeper channels, while many additional species of shorebirds and waterfowl tap the food supply at various other levels, each finding its own feeding niche in accordance with its particular adaptations.

This is the ancient balance, a balance of supply and demand, a balance of numbers, a diverse, living system of close associations and dependencies. As we explore the lagoon and learn the ways of the birds, we begin to understand the importance of Audubon Canyon Ranch as a surviving piece of wilderness. For each of us the Ranch becomes a place where we can glimpse the mainstream of evolution, where we can experience a moment in the lives of other creatures with which we share this planet. It is a place to breathe the same air that they breathe, to bask in the same sun or shiver in the same fog. It is a place to reckon with the fact that we also need sun, soil, water, air, and green things growing; that we depend upon the same immense, beautifully balanced system of relationships that sustains everything alive, for if we share the gift of life, we realize, so we must also share the means of living.

Besides what the garden provides, students who stay with us in the canyon harvest some foods from among the edible plants that grow wild around us. Salads are made from purslane, miner's lettuce, watercress, and mustard blossoms. Stinging nettles are boiled and chopped for soups or omelets, and cattail shoots or blossoms are picked when the time is right. The students learn that once, not so many decades ago, this place was an Indian campsite, and the hills and rich lagoon provided all the food and shelter they needed.

It always proves interesting to remind the students that, in addition to fruit and milk sugars, the average American now consumes over one hundred pounds of refined sugar a year, and to ask them what sources of sweets native Americans were once able to find in the local environment. There were no fields of cane or sugar beets, no peaches, apricots, dates, or apples, not even any good sugar maple trees, though a low-grade sap can be extracted from the maples that line our stream. There were not even honeybees, for these industrious gatherers of sweet nectar had not yet been brought from their European homeland.

The Indians must have relied solely upon wild grapes, currants, and various other kinds of berries that grow in our region. When we take students with us to forage for huckleberries or wild strawberries, they quickly appreciate the length of time required to harvest these tiny fruits. Furthermore, they realize that the berry season is short and that much extra would have had to be dried and stored for the tribe to have had occasional winter sweets.

What food the canyon itself does not provide for our visiting students we purchase in bulk for the week. We carefully select wholesome, healthful foods and figure on several meatless meals so that the students will be exposed to various sources of protein. Just as few young people have ever made bread, so we have also discovered that few have cooked a meal. At the Ranch we cook only the first couple of meals, using no recipes; after that the students plan and cook the rest. Before the week has ended, they have caught the flavor of the adventure, and creative, spontaneous meals emerge that would surprise the best of chefs. We all cook and eat together, for mealtime provides a joyous meeting on common ground.

Occasionally we hear from parents after the students have returned home from a stay at the Ranch. The reports sometimes tell of how the dissection of scat or the preparation of skeletons first emerged as a topic of conversation at the dinner table. But most often the immediate changes parents notice in their children have to do with food. They ask for carrots or nuts in their lunch bags instead of candy; they insist on altering the weekly shopping list, and now and then they ask to cook a meal or bake some bread.

Perhaps the most significant thing the students learn from participating in our way of life is the importance of an entire process rather than results alone. Too much schooling is founded upon a system in which the end is more important than the means. There are no grades to strive for when students visit the Ranch. Even the quality of a meal or a loaf of bread is less important than the excite-

ment, the satisfaction, and the knowledge gained in preparing it.

Another experience that Maggie shares with the students is spinning yarn. She has wool sheared from her sheep and piles of dog hair ready for spinning, and while some students work at the wheel, others harvest leaves, flowers, or roots for brewing dyes. Once the yarn is spun and some of it colored, the students make their own weaving tools and set about translating the materials they have made into works of art. The results are often spectacular, but they can never compare with the sense of fulfillment that has been gained through the process itself. The end results we can see, while the joy of the process may be expressed only through a word or a glint in a student's eye, and often it remains silent within. Teaching is like gardening; one learns that seeds once planted do not make instant trees. But someday there is shade and fruit, and the world is made more gentle by their presence.

When students live with us for a week, each day is filled with activity, for there is much we want to explore. We learn what it means to work together on projects of common interest, but we discover also the need to be alone. This discovery especially the students cherish, for here they *can* be alone. There is no radio, no television. No cars are allowed in or out of the canyon. There are no demands except those we place upon ourselves. We are left to our own resources, and the students find perhaps the strongest of these by being alone.

So as the days go by, evenings become more important. When evening comes and the dinner chores have been completed, there is a natural coming together. A warm campfire draws the tribal needs from within us, and the tribe gathers. No two evenings are alike. Sometimes we sing, sometimes we talk, and once in a while, by unspoken agreement, we are simply quiet.

I remember one evening in particular when the music tradition began. Maggie has a guitar, and students often bring instruments of their own. But this night around the fire was different. One girl had stumbled upon a stand of giant horsetails growing in an isolated draw. She had learned that the stems could be pulled apart into sections, open at one end and closed by a membrane at the other. Furthermore, she knew that the sections were of different lengths and that, if assembled in a graduated manner, could be fashioned into a fine set of whistles like the Pipes of Pan. This instrument she proudly unveiled before the group, and thus began a rare and beautiful evening.

Maggie brought out a goatskin drum she had made from an old wine cask; one of the research associates surfaced with a Jamaican rumba box she had made; I found some rattle gourds I had grown in the garden; and the rest of the tribe played a varied assortment of kitchen utensils. Making music was no longer restricted to the "musicians." From one and all, the great music flowed.

Sometimes students want to be alone with their music and go off by themselves at dusk or early morning to play quietly in the silence of the canyon, with only the calls of birds for accompaniment. There is no describing the sound of a flute or a muted trombone drifting through the canyon on a quiet night. At times like these music becomes more

than music, both for those who create it and for those who listen from afar. It becomes a spiritual experience, reaching to the depths of one's soul.

Once a girl brought her bagpipes to the canyon, and by day we often reveled in their joy and good humor. There is something about bagpipes at close range that makes one want to laugh, dance, and scream all at the same time, but at night, when the sound came alone from far off beyond the moonlit marsh, we felt transported to the moors of Scotland, where the clan might have been gathering in a distant village.

The pipes sang an eerie and beautiful song. For me they filled yet another void, for they reminded me of my travels in India more than a decade ago. In that distant land of rural people, homemade music is a mainstay of life. Wherever we camped, even in the wildest regions, the soft sounds of music drifted upon the night breeze. I had forgotten how important a link they provided with our fellow man through the darkness. I had forgotten even that I missed them here where music too often must be plucked from the silent air by electrical contrivance.

These various musical interludes that occurred when students were visiting established another interesting link between the past, the natural world, and our life in the canyon. It began purely as a natural history investigation in the marsh.

During the summer we found a number of enormous green caterpillars feeding on the alders. In order to be certain of their identity, I raised a few of them in a cage, and eventually they spun cocoons. It was not until the dead of winter that we were able to appreciate how many caterpillars there had been in the trees, so camouflaged had they been among the leaves. When the alders were bare, we could easily spot over ten dozen huge silver cocoons attached to the branches.

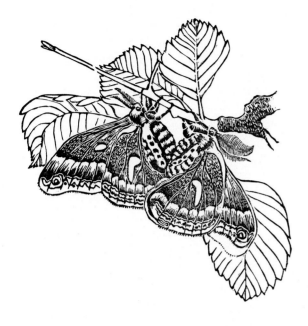

On May 11 of our second spring, one of the cocoons in my rearing cage produced a magnificent cecropia moth, and during the next few days several more emerged. By that time the alders were in full leaf again, and it was nearly impossible to watch for the emergence of those left on the trees.

One morning I found a female cecropia just crawling from its cocoon. I decided to try an experiment. Before its wings had even expanded, I gently transported the moth to the marsh and placed it on the branch of an alder. Soon its wings had been pumped with fluids until they were full size, and the remarkable patterns of earth-colored scales gleamed in the sunlight.

I know that female cecropias, heavy of body and laden with eggs, are rather sedentary, and I suspected that the moth would remain where I had put her until nightfall. I also knew that they, like their close relatives, the polyphemus moths, emit chemicals called pheromones in order to attract a mate. The males of these species are equipped with spectacular plumose antennae with which they are able to detect as little as a single pheromone molecule and to follow the chemical along a gradient of increasing concentration for distances of several miles toward the females that produce them. This system of sex attraction is certainly one of the most remarkable wonders of the natural world; how it evolved will perhaps forever remain an intriguing mystery.

Early the next morning I went again to the marsh and checked the tree. Sure enough, there was the female, and with her, locked in copulation, was a male. I watched the pair off and on during the day, and at nightfall they were still mating, unmoved from their morning perch. By the second morning both moths were gone, but in their place and all around the vicinity on leaves and twigs were numerous large red eggs. Another generation had begun.

Once all the moths in my rearing cage had emerged and been released, Maggie set about cleaning the cage. As she was doing so, she decided to take a close look at the cocoons. With a pair of scissors she slit one open and folded the halves back. What an incredible design for survival!

The empty pupal case and the last-shed skin of the caterpillar were neatly encased by a soft, inner cocoon. Next, there was a loose webwork of silk arranged to provide a thick insulating air space, and the whole inner structure was surrounded by a tight, waterproof coat of silk so tough that we could not tear it.

We thought again of all those cocoons in the winter-bare alders, fully exposed to wind, driving rain, and icy cold. Here before us we saw the reason the cecropias could persist in the face of these difficult odds. The cecropia belongs to the silk moth family, and we wondered how many hundreds, or even thousands, of yards of silk thread the caterpilar had had to spin in order to construct this superb weatherproof wrapping. We also wondered how the big moths, which are soft-bodied and have no chewing mouthparts, were able to emerge from these tough, parchmentlike cocoons. We studied them carefully and found that the caterpillar leaves an opening in the silk at the pointed end of the tear-shaped case. But the hole was tightly closed by the silk which when dry pulls together like a drawstring bag. One of the recently vacated cocoons was damp, however, and close examination of this one revealed that the emerging moth softens the silk with body fluids that enable it to expand the opening and thus crawl free. As the empty cocoon dries again, this marvelously contrived exit draws tightly closed just as though nothing at all had happened!

Our curiosity satisfied, we were about to throw the old cocoons away when Maggie remembered both the music fests with our students and something she had read about Indian crafts. Many tribes of California Indians used cecropia cocoons to make rattles as part of their repertoire of musical instruments. What had begun as a spontaneous lesson in evolution and survival became in that instant an equally spontaneous impetus for creative expression. We set the cocoons aside for the construction of a rattle, feeling fulfilled that once again a connection had been made between our life and our natural surroundings.

Since then Maggie has also made clackers from elderberry stalks designed after those once used by Indians of the region, and during subsequent evenings around the fire stick xylophones, bone chimes, and many other instruments have been fashioned with students on the spur of the moment. Thus the music tradition continues.

The best evenings of all around the fire, however, are those that prompt quiet discussion. Especially toward the end of a week together, when the students face the prospect of leaving, they begin asking those searching questions that give life its greatest substance. Sometimes they strive to express what they have felt or what they have learned; sometimes they probe deeply for the meaning of what Maggie and I have learned in our own small part of a lifetime, and sometimes they grope for answers to the unanswerable questions that have followed the spirits of men since the dawn of our species. Their young minds search within for

questions far older than they, and we explore together at the fringes of man's experience, sharing in the one thing which, if any, draws people together, and that is an expression of the spirit. These moments emerge, as they have throughout history, by being allowed to, and we all know ourselves and each other better because of them.

Time and time again young people have asked us how we arrived at our way of life, how we found work that we love and a home that we cherish, and, for that matter, how we found each other. Few who know us, least of all those students who are with us for a week or less, have had a chance to experience the long hours, the toil, the agonizing decisions, the compromises, and the long, slow growth that lie behind what they see as the simple life. They experience only the peace, the joy, and the generally happy bickering that grace most of our days. By good fortune, exposure to those qualities of living is the best place for anyone to begin his own search. They are goals enough to strive for in life. We ourselves began with them, and we have kept them always in sight. But the long road getting there is another matter. This road we have just begun to travel, and we can only answer the questions posed to us by describing what small part of the geography we have seen thus far.

Often this evening sharing revolves around our creative work and the question of earning a living, which looms large before young people in the throes of preparing themselves for life. We explain in answer to their questions that in a sense our way of life has come about through adaptation. Just as the shrubs of the chaparral have become adapted for drought by developing deep roots while the redwoods are ready with surface roots to receive the fog drip of summer, so we have tried to be ready for opportunities as well as problems by developing the various skills necessary for our own survival.

Man has a heritage not as ancient as that of the redwood but equally impressive in its evolutionary achievements. We have been given in our genes some powerful tools for survival, the most unique of which is our mind. Unlike the redwood, we do not have to accept as fate whatever circumstances present themselves. We can affect the world just as surely as that world can affect us. More than any other organism on earth, we have freedom of choice.

For Maggie and me, developing a livelihood has been a natural evolution of choice. We have weighed opportunities carefully and selected those that fit our skills as they have grown and our convictions as they have formed. We have tried always to reject whatever we felt we could not accomplish with integrity and whatever we could not believe in honestly.

Our lives, separately and together, have evolved by cause and effect. My childhood interest in the things of nature led to numerous jobs, both at home and abroad, in the out-of-doors. These experiences in turn led me to photography, and photography quite by chance led to writing. Maggie had a long-developing interest in the psychic needs of man. Almost by accident she stumbled upon biology in college. These combined interests and her natural gift with children and animals led eventually to teaching and, more recently, to an exploration of arts and crafts.

Through our mutual interests we found each other, and our experiences together led us toward teaching as a livelihood. Neither of us had had any formal training in education; teaching simply evolved from our love of the natural world and our love of children. In one sense our life together has simply happened, but in another sense we have made it happen through the careful, often painstaking use of choice. Perhaps our greatest rewards have come through learning to work together in a spirit of sharing rather than competition.

Creativity is a lonely process. Insight and creative expression, even when they arise from group interaction, emerge from the singular sensitivity man has to his individuality and aloneness in this world. These are internal, personal happenings felt only by the one at that instant touched by them; they can be shared, but only in retrospect. For us the beauty of teaching lies in the fact that this sharing is most often immediate rather than deferred. By exploring together, there always exists the possibility that a moment of discovery will spark that magic chain reaction in which feelings or ideas flow quickly from person to person. It is an electrical occurrence that sets into motion some of man's most powerful energies, and it can only happen when individuals have an opportunity to interact directly, face to face.

Learning, like a fire, must be tended carefully. A certain kindling temperature must be reached to ignite the process. Too many people together, like too much fuel packed tightly without sufficient air, stifle the fires of learning or prevent their ignition altogether. On the other hand, if the flames burn brightly both long and often, all the fuel is consumed. Good learning is at once an invigorating and exhausting process from which the mind must frequently escape for renewal.

We have tried to strike this balance by working with small numbers on a part-time basis. Between sessions with students we return to the routine, physical processes of living, which allow the mind to idle, and we return also to the kinds of creative expression that tend to synthesize the very substance of what we stand for as individuals. Both seem to provide the experiences that in turn feed a vital teaching situation.

Writing, photography, and many other art forms require solitary execution and even longer periods of solitary rumination. I have often taught photography classes, and even then, except for an occasional bottom protruding from the grass, we seldom see each other until we gather to share our results. Unlike teaching, the actual work and exploration in these fields are not matters for group interaction.

Besides the need to earn a livelihood, the desire to communicate does however, lie behind our sharing of art and writing. After all, the first cave paintings and the first written tablets were rendered as a means to communicate. Art and the written word have become man's most potent tools of communication, particularly as the numbers and geographical spread of our species have grown to encompass the entire planet. But from the very beginning these forms of expression have served a deeper function still. They are tools for honing one's personal statement: this is who I am; this is what I believe.

Here lies the deepest loneliness of man. Beyond the spoken word or directly shared skills that define most people's place in this world, there is no immediate audience, there are no eyes to reflect the fires of recognition or learning, especially now that communication of art and writing has spread so far beyond the family or the tribe. Most of the seeds that one casts will germinate in soil where he will never set foot. The only chain reaction that one can experience is internal. By this alone the writer or the artist must take his major bearings in life.

The union of creative work and family life is not easily accomplished. The lengthy periods of mental solitude that creativity requires must be obtained at the exclusion of other people, even members of one's own family. When one is so engaged, other members of the family may not be. When we are together at such times, Maggie and I have discovered that we often do not even hear each other. We might as well be in different worlds.

Raising a young child during these periods of creative involvement is especially difficult. Children have instant needs, both mental and physical, which cannot be deferred, and the burden of meeting these needs must fall to the other parent. When we are both engaged in creative work at the same time, Pippin suffers most, having no accessible extended family most of the time and few neighbors to cover for our temporary lack of availability. On the other hand, we have observed that at such times, thrust on his own, Pippin will often go off by himself and engage in his own creative pursuits, an opportunity seldom available to children in this age of hyperinvolvement. Therefore he seems to be developing an acute sense of self-awareness and expression, and a respect for the needs of others. When we come together again as a family, we try to share in the joy of our own growth as well as of Pippin's.

Occasional periods of creative work, added to the routine of subsistence living and periodic stints of teaching, have also brought to our lives the strain of unpredictability. Though teaching programs and the best date to plant onions are events that can be planned and marked on a calendar, there is no way to predict when pests will invade the garden or when the creative urge will consume us. This, too, however, may be a blessing in disguise, for dealing with sudden change is part of the challenge as well as the adventure of being alive with all our senses. Life is not flat; it has topography no matter how smooth we try to make it, and the ability to shift gears quickly and without trauma may be necessary for survival even under the best of circumstances.

It is this rhythm actually, asymmetrical as it often seems, which is one of the most significant outgrowths of our search for a way of life parallel to our inner nature. Our work has become our way of life, and our way of life has in turn become our work. We carry our job with us. Since life is no longer divided, much energy is saved. The one endeavor feeds the other, and together both can grow. Mental stimulation draws us back to the simple acts of living. Being with people in time creates the need to be alone. And the loneliness of creative expression sooner or later attracts us once more to the vitality of group interaction and the immediacy of sharing that we find in teaching.

It has been rewarding to learn to work together in a spirit of sharing rather than competition. This sharing, at times both free and employed, has drawn us particularly close. This closeness, in turn, has affected our attitude toward teaching.

This is not teaching in the usual sense of the word but rather in a sense far older and more akin with our beginnings as a species. It is not exactly the teaching of a body of knowledge, though the importance of knowledge cannot be denied. It is instead a sharing of skills with which we can better communicate with our inner selves and the world around us. It is living itself, shared in the act and expressed in the broadest sense of joy and awareness and sensitivity. We serve an apprenticeship with others at the same time they serve an apprentice-ship with us, and when the moments of learning occur, we rejoice.

Jung defined this process of sharing by saying, "The gifts of the heart are not quite so obvious or as impressive as intellectual and technical endow-ments, and, just as the latter demand special under-standing from the teacher, so these other gifts often make the even greater demand that he him-self should be educated. For the day will inevitably come when what the educator teaches by word of mouth no longer works, but only what he is."

In the history of man, that day once prevailed. We have only to find it again.

5

FRIENDS

One day a man came to talk about buying some photographs. I sat him down outside in the sun beside a large mound of fava beans, and while we discussed the project, we shelled the whole pile. Another time a friend spent the weekend for a relaxing change in the country; together we built a hundred yards of trail in the canyon. So it often goes with visitors on the farm.

We find it difficult to define where our work ends and play begins, so integrated are they in daily life. Visitors who spend only a short time with us most often leave with the impression that we work nearly all the time, but the truth is rather that we are nearly always *busy*.

It is often equally difficult for us to distinguish students from friends, for many of those who have studied with us have become our closest friends, and many friends have become students. Furthermore, we are as much their students as they are ours, and so the whole question in most cases becomes irrelevant.

The old precept of not mixing business with pleasure holds little meaning for us. There is much to be gained from sharing freely across the boundaries that have become traditional definitions of the

use of time. A moment of learning, inspiration, or joy can occur as readily in work as in play or relaxation, for time and people are continuums that yield less of the essential spark of life when confined in boxes.

Still, the division of work from recreation and of office from home does provide a handy protection of privacy and solitude, and the lack of this feature in our free-lance, work-at-home way of life has raised some problems with which we have had to deal. During our first summer we were overwhelmed with friends and acquaintances who wanted to spend a day in the country. We have always enjoyed visitors, and for a while we managed by putting them to work. In this way we were able to continue the essential routines around the place and visit at the same time. Maggie is a willing cook, and I enjoy helping in the kitchen, so a pleasant meal together usually rounded out the day's activities.

As time passed, however, we became increasingly disturbed by two important realizations. First, the more deeply we became involved in our creative work, the more we understood our need for solitude and tranquillity. Visiting over a pile of fava beans was fine as far as shelling the beans was concerned, for many hands make light work of routine chores. But when shelling beans, cutting wood, or weeding the garden served as a quiet time of rumination, doing the chores and visiting were not so often compatible. We began to see that for every hour we spent writing, drawing, or teaching, we needed many hours more of quiet busywork during which our creative energies could be recharged. Incubation time is rare in our culture. We were finding it again and discovering its essential qualities.

In addition, we found that while human contact is important beyond measure, every person has a certain maximum capacity for it. I read somewhere once that for every new friend gained an old one must be shed. In many ways this must be true. A person's spiritual energy is finite, even though that energy may grow or change with time. We found that the more people we spent time with, the less energy we had for any of them. This troubled us deeply, for we have never taken human contact lightly. At last we had to make some important decisions.

The first thing we did was acquire an unlisted telephone number, for the phone had long been an invasion of the continuity of our time. Over the years, we had gained a reputation as a source of free advice regarding matters of the natural world. At any hour of the day or night we could expect an inquiry about giving a talk to a community group, supporting a conservation measure, accepting a teaching job, or properly caring for an orphaned bird. A woman even called late one night to ask if she should treat her sick turtle by brushing its teeth!

The phone, when you stop to think about it, is a highly insistent and in many ways selfish means of communication. Inherent in the telephone is the feeling that the party at the other end must be of a mind to accept a question or message entirely at the caller's discretion. As we gave ourselves up to the natural flow of our life at the Ranch, we found ourselves less and less able to do business on the spur of the moment at someone else's insistence. In time, our resentment of telephone interruptions grew, and had we not needed the phone for occasional Ranch business or possible emergencies, we would have eliminated it entirely. An unlisted number seemed a fair compromise.

We let it be known that we preferred to communicate by mail, for a letter written and a letter answered can both be executed with greater care and thought, and at a moment convenient to both parties.

This was to some degree an innocent move, for we never dreamed of the stir it would cause. Countless people were miffed, even incensed, that we refused to be instantly available. We realized more than ever before how the telephone has changed communication across the distance of space by removing the distance of time.

In order to secure some quiet time for writing, the next move we made was to lock the front gate and hang from it a sign that said, ENTRANCE BY APPOINTMENT ONLY. Though the gate had always been there, we had never used it. We must hardly even have noticed it, for when it was closed, we were surprised at the imposing barrier it presented. We assumed that the gate and sign together would suggest that we were busy and did not wish to be disturbed.

The first day of our experiment I settled into my grandfather's old morris chair and began some long neglected writing. Before the day had ended, three people had bothered to vault the high gate in order to come for a visit. When asked if they had noticed the sign, they all replied that they assumed it applied to someone else!

We had met one of these people briefly before, found we had much in common, and established a

friendship through correspondence during two years he and his wife spent travelling and studying in Europe. Our letters meant much in terms of personal growth on both sides of the Atlantic. When they returned to see us in our new home at the Ranch, we shared in person as we had shared by mail. But that particular day the fellow came to visit and discovered that the gate was locked. When he reached the house, he found me deeply engrossed in writing, and I asked if he might not come again at a time of mutual convenience. He was outraged. "First I find that I cannot call you, and now I find a lock on the gate," he exclaimed. "What about the mail?" I ventured, but it was apparent that the distance between us and San Francisco meant something quite different to him than the distance between us and Europe. He left in a huff, and we have never seen or heard from him since.

Closing the gate proved to be the final screen that separated the fine grains of humanity from the coarse. Many were angry indeed that they had driven all the way to the country (without notice) to see us and found the gate locked. As time passed, however, those who knew us accepted, with or without understanding, our creative needs and adjusted accordingly. Out of this process of selection have emerged our truest friends, for they alone realize that friendship, except in times of genuine need, is not dependent upon immediate or even frequent renewal.

During the months that followed the hanging of the sign, the canyon grew quieter, and we found new strength in the resulting peacefulness and continuity of our time. We also found that we had more energy to share with our friends. Our contacts with people, though less frequent, grew richer because they were precious, because we all took the encounter seriously, in work or play, and made the most of it.

During this seemingly brutal selective process, we learned another significant lesson. There are those people in the world who give as well as take, who recharge and replenish one's energy, and there are also those whose needs are so great that they drain one nearly dry. Maggie and I, by sharing ourselves freely, have been renewed and strengthened by the former but have also been vulnerable to the latter. We have been many years developing the ability to say no, and the small physical act of hanging a sign on the gate has strangely given us courage to say no with greater understanding.

No is the simplest and most potent word in any language, next to *I*. To say it with meaning requires much knowledge of oneself and respect for the person to whom it is directed. With regard to raising children, *no* is perhaps the most abused of all words, and we carry with us into adulthood the resulting scars. We use the word either too often or not enough, but almost always idly. To say no to another person, most of all a friend or a loved one, is as vital as saying yes and carries with it at least as much responsibility.

Learning to say no is the most important part of learning to tread lightly upon the world. Like Don Juan told Carlos Castañeda in *Journey to Ixtlan*, one must learn to use one's world "sparingly and with tenderness, regardless of whether the world might be things, or plants, or animals, or people, or power."

"You must learn to become deliberately available and unavailable," Don Juan advised. "It makes no difference to hide if everyone knows that you are hiding. To be unavailable means that you deliberately avoid exhausting yourself and others. You don't use and squeeze people until they have shriveled to nothing, especially the people you love."

The gate may stay open now, but few venture past it without having written first. We are less often exhausted, and when friends do visit, our wellspring of energy is more often filled again than drained. Slowly we are learning to treat the world, our friends, and ourselves sparingly.

In America it used to be that communities of common geography were the rule rather than the exception. One's community consisted of neighboring farm families or members of the village or the small town. As cities have spread across the land, however, and our mobility has increased, the concept of community has been stretched to include far distant points of geography, its boundaries defined in terms of where one's closest friends and associates reside, regardless of the space between. It is a phenomenon of cities that one can live a lifetime in one spot and never know one's neighbors.

When we first moved to Audubon Canyon Ranch, our immediate community included people from all over the county as well as from the larger San Francico Bay Area, and to a great extent it still does. We ourselves were raised in this urban environment, and most of our friends and those who come to the Ranch as students and visitors are urban people. As rural ways have gradually overcome Maggie and me, humorous differences have surfaced between our life-style and capability and those of our friends.

Many of them shake their heads in amazement at our inability to cope with even the most basic aspects of twentieth-century living.

My own checking account record has not been accurately balanced for five years. It has become an expectation among friends that when we arrive at a meeting or social function there is sure to be some detail amiss with our appearance. We may be completedly dressed for town with the singular exception that we have left the farm with our mud boots on, that I have forgotten to shave, that Maggie has gone off with bread flour still on her face where she scratched her nose, or that I have forgotten to check myself for smudges of soot left from stoking the wood stove. We resist leaving the country for any reason, even occasional necessity, and our friends long ago gave up worrying that, lacking television, we should at least join them periodically for a restaurant dinner and an evening at the theater or the symphony.

We were not always so much in tune with rural living. Even though we made our transition from town in gradual steps, we had a great deal to learn and made numerous mistakes. I shall not forget the day I wore my first brand new pair of overalls —"Farmer Johns," as Maggie calls them. Donning an old straw hat to top off the image, I drove the Ranch tractor proudly to the local service station to fill its tank with gas. I wondered why people looked at me so strangely; it was not until I made a visit to the rest room that I discovered I had put my overalls on backwards! Later in the morning, while cutting the grass beneath the apple trees with the tractor's big rotary mower, my hat caught on a low-hanging limb, fell beneath the blades, and was quickly added to the fodder. So much for the country farmer's image.

Still, as we have grown more adept at living close to the land, we have had frequent opportunity to see our old urban ways with new perspective. When city folk come to visit, they are more often than not quite out of their element. A large party of New Yorkers arrived in the canyon one day, having made arrangements to photograph an airline commercial in the house, "for a little flavor of nineteenth-century America," as they put it. On our handmade dining table, against a wall of old furniture and a ninety-year-old quilt that once belonged to my great-grandmother, a couple of "passengers" were served the typical space-age airline meals. Some of the accessories had been left behind, and we were first asked for a plastic cup, which we didn't have. Then they needed sugar for the coffee, but we had only honey. Next they asked for milk, to which Maggie replied that, yes, we did have milk, but they would have to wait a few minutes until she got some from the goat. And so it went through the day.

With the exception of special celebrations, the meals Maggie serves are no more elaborately made when we have guests than when we are alone. The food we eat, which seems matter-of-course to us and takes no more and often less time to prepare

than more conventional fare, seems exotic to most people, if only because it is home grown and spontaneously put together.

Nowhere has the difference in our way of life become more clear than in the vegetable department. We enjoy giving visitors some of our extra garden produce to take home with them, but we find that few people indeed have the slightest idea what to do with leeks, parsnips, or celeriac, and fewer still have even heard of kohlrabi, chicory, or broccolini.

On the other hand, it warms our hearts to walk through the garden with people of our parents' generation or older, for many of them grew up on farms and almost cry from pleasant memories raised by the smell of a vine-ripe tomato or fresh basil, the sight of rutabagas or ground cherries. We often wonder why they gave up so much of what they loved.

When Maggie and I decided to make a change in our way of life without entirely leaving the urban culture from which we came, we could only approximate in our minds what the results of our decision would be. Our experience thus far tells us that living the simple life close to a metropolis is a mixed blessing.

The San Francisco Bay Area has long been known as a haunt for creative people and a seedbed for new ideas. On the surface, the towns and suburbs that sprawl together in a great, encompassing metropolitan embrace are as faceless as the rest of urban America, but underneath run strong, exciting currents of change. The Bay Area contains an especially rich aggregation of people who have come from every walk of life and from nearly every corner of the world. They have brought with them what, in sum, is the widest possible assortment of talents, ideas, and points of view.

As a functioning, integrated society, this collection of humanity is far from perfect. The rich have plenty, which they refuse to relinquish, while the poor have little and clamor for more. And yet, in spite of it all, or perhaps because of it, values are slowly changing. They are speaking, if only from a different vantage, of the same goal—upgrading the quality of life. Though the poles of humanity are still miles, even worlds, apart, the people of this region at least give each other voice. However plugged are the ears of change, the many voices nevertheless are dimly heard. In this sense, the life of democracy still flickers.

Living in proximity to this ferment of social change is a tremendously stimulating experience. Our friends are all, one way or another, participating, just as we are by following our own convictions. When they visit us or we visit them, our minds bend, we are renewed, and Pippin is exposed to interesting people and varied experiences. It is impossible to live in a vacuum where the winds of change blow so strongly all around.

But what is the function of a community? Those we know and love, and those with whom we work are scattered all over the map. Is it enough that we gather now and then at the election booth or the signing of a petition, in a store, or even over a stimulating discussion?

This is where we have felt the greatest void. Friends come and chop a little wood or pull a few weeds in the garden and then go away again. Who is there to help build a chicken house and to ask our help in return? Where are the people with whom to share a common way of life? Is this common bond not the heartbeat of a community?

As long as our energy was spread far and wide, among distant people and diverse causes, we had little left to explore the community possibilities among neighbors and residents of the local villages. Gradually, however, we have begun this process, first by patronizing local shops, then by trading ideas and skills with the nearest neighbors. We have found that many of those who live in our immediate area are, like ourselves, refugees from the city seeking a new life on the fringe, where they can experience what Joseph Wood Krutch has called "the best of two worlds."

Some who visit us from town have been moved toward making some basic changes in their own ways of living. They ask our advice about growing vegetables, and with just a little encouragement added to the dissatisfaction they have felt over

high prices and processed foods, they tear out their junipers, rip up their lawns, and plant a garden. The garden provides more than produce; it becomes a focal point for the family, even the neighborhood. Small as it may seem, this is the manner in which gentle revolutions begin, and we are more than pleased to play even a minute role in the process. But sharing across an expanse of geography is no substitute for a community founded upon common local needs.

The two villages that lie on either side of us are not even remotely self-sufficient communities. The Big Town lies too near; it meets our needs too easily. But common problems such as water supply, sewage treatment, population density, and environmental protection have begun to draw the villagers together. Perhaps the time will come when we all see that we share common needs beyond those that are forced upon us, needs that simply have to do with creating a richer, more self-sufficient way of life, which gives us common meeting ground and from which we can all benefit. The seeds of mutual cooperation have been sown here and there among us, as they have been in countless settlements across the land. Whether in cities or in the countryside, if genuine communities can rise again from the fragmented American landscape, we shall experience the most profound and constructive of all revolutions.

Recreation used to be utilitarian or, at the very least, a continuation of the learning process. Before white men arrived in America, tribal gatherings had great significance. They were joyous rites of renewal in which a vision was shared or an idea expressed, in which rain was called forth from the heavens or a successful hunt was celebrated that it might happen again. Even as the pioneers settled westward across the continent, barn raisings, corn shuckings, and quilting bees became traditional communal ways of making light, happy work of necessary chores. A rousting barn dance was a means of bonding a community together, an occasion of meeting and sharing.

The coming together of people for common enjoyment strengthens human bonds and the sense of community. For countless centuries people grew in skill and creative expression, defined family and community roles, and experienced joy of lasting quality through shared recreation. Now we buy most of our recreation, but we have not entirely replaced through purchase the satisfaction we once achieved through our own spontaneous efforts.

In the tribe and in the village, one of the most important human needs fulfilled by communal sharing is the need for celebration. Even though our communities have largely been scattered and only now are being born again, our need to celebrate has not been lost. Needs can be suppressed just so long before they bubble to the surface, seeking release through whatever cracks they can find in the hardened crust that civilization plasters over them in its attempt to hide or mold the human spirit. We still need to unwind, to play, and to have fun. We still need to seek wisdom in a spirit of joy and goodwill. We still need to laugh, and we have not lost the need for each other. Just as people have begun to seek new functions where old ones have failed them, so many have also begun to search again for more meaningful forms of companionship.

Societies are like trees; when a branch becomes unhealthy, it is discarded. New sprouts appear lower down, farther back toward the source of energy, and they grow vigorously toward the sunlight. Whether of limbs or ideas or modes of behavior, this is the natural process of pruning. It is the original rite of renewal.

One autumn day near Halloween, when we still lived in our tiny San Geronimo Valley cabin, we asked in some friends, gathered together the neighborhood children, and began carving pumpkins. Not one pumpkin, or a few, or even pumpkins alone, but squash from the garden by the dozens, of every size and description. Thus the Pumpkin Celebration was born.

As our first autumn at Audubon Canyon Ranch approached a year later, the same feeling rose again within us, but we were too busy with practical matters to acknowledge it. When the leaves began turning gold the second year, however, the joy of the harvest could no longer be suppressed. Each morning as the air grew clear and crisp, I felt myself drawn to the squash patch as if called by some ancient, magic incantation. At last they were ready for harvest, and I began loading them into the wheelbarrow. There were little ones and huge ones, long ones and flat ones. Some were red, some orange, some striped with green and yellow, and some were a soft blue green. There were varieties from Japan and China, some from Africa and Europe, and others that were cultivated by the Mayans in Central America long ago.

I wheeled them down to the house, load after load, a thousand pounds or more. Our tastiest favorites, those that would feed us during the winter, Maggie and I piled around the corners of the dining room. The rest we set aside in a huge pile, a great heaping legacy of thousands of years of cultivation and selection by untold generations of farmers. The lines of descent converged here in this many-colored, multi-formed pile of plenty, the fruits of an ancient plant-and-man cooperative. There was no question in our minds; it was time again for the Pumpkin Celebration.

We set the date for the week before Halloween, sent invitations to our friends, and asked for an RSVP by mail. Almost every response came back in the form of a beautiful handmade note of acceptance, a spontaneous work of art.

A few days ahead of time, one of the little goat kids was slaughtered and hung to cure, and a large roasting pit was dug in the garden. Maggie began baking tasty morsels and placing them in the pantry. Apples were picked, squeezed in the press, and the juice set aside to become cider.

On the morning of October 22, little Pippin helped me build a log fire in the roasting pit. We took the goat kid to the house, rubbed it down with garlic and butter, and filled its body cavity with fresh potatoes, onions, kohlrabis, and spices from the garden. While Maggie laced the body closed, Pippin and I made a spicy marinade and constructed a swabbing brush by tying four kinds of mint sprigs to a willow stick. We anchored the legs of the goat securely to a long green alder pole cut from the marsh and carried it back to the garden, placing it over the glowing coals in the roasting pit. This was our offering of sustenance from the animal kingdom.

Next we selected our largest banana squash, cut off one end, scooped out the seeds, and coated the inside with molasses. Into the cavity Maggie packed

a mixture of baked beans, gingered pears, and pineapple, fastened the cut end in place with splinters of wood, wrapped the whole squash in a cradle of wire mesh, and placed it over the coals beside the goat. Into the hot oven Maggie placed several dozen crisp autumn apples stuffed with nuts and raisins. These were our offering from the vegetable kingdom.

By the time friends and neighbors began to arrive, the canyon was filled with the sweet aromas of roasting meat, mulled wine, and hot spiced apple cider. It was a grand gathering. We carved pumpkins and squash all day, kids and adults alike, and in a while Pippin and some of the other youngsters took leave of the squash pile to play with the goats, climb the Great Buckeye, or blow soap bubbles through baling wire hoops.

While we carved and ate and drank, we visited, mostly about ordinary things, for this was not a day for profound words but rather one for profound feelings. It was a day to be children, to do what we had not done for many years, perhaps even for generations. And always, underneath the surface of the day, ran that ancient current that rose up from the very youth of our species. The goat, simmering whole over the coals, was new to our experience, but something about it was a part of us, and all day people drifted one by one to the roasting pit to swab it with sauce and turn it to another side.

As time passed, a strange phenomenon was noticed by all. The squash being carved began to assume great character. Traditional round pumpkins haven't a great deal to offer; the faces always seem to look about the same. But this heap of cucurbits were at least as varied as the artists behind the knives, and their inherent characteristics seemed to strike a different spark in those who worked them. Some were meticulous and controlled; some were wild and happy, almost bacchanalian; others were sinister and sly. Differences were recognizable also between those faces carved by children and those designed by grown-ups. The expressions conceived by children, though often rendered with less skill, were the freest and most spontaneous. Children we were that day, one and all, but the complexities of adulthood were recorded nevertheless as surely as an earthquake registers on a seismograph.

Late in the afternoon the feast was spread among us. We ate until the bones of the goat and the skin of the squash were all that remained. As evening embraced the canyon, the pumpkins beckoned, and we assembled around them.

All the squash people were placed together three tiers high on tables and benches, and a candle placed in each. Everyone was quiet now as a sense of solemnity enveloped us. As though by command, the great horned owls began to hoot back and forth across the ranch yard, and the bats emerged from wall spaces and attics to begin their nightly hunt. When the last dusk light had vanished, we struck our matches and lit the candles until all the squash people were alive as only the ancient spark of fire can make them.

We stood before them, silent and transfixed. Our faces glowed with their flickering orange light until it was no longer easy to know with any certainty which faces were really human and which were mere reflections of humanity. In that eerie flame-lit moment there was a great blending of spirit and countenance. It was as though the whole species was marching before us in a pagan procession. Among the faces, both those staring in and those staring out, were the happiest and the most sorrowful, the gentlest and the meanest, the most benevolent and the most wicked of all men, for there is a little of them all in each of us and in each of our creations.

A long time passed, or so it seemed, until finally someone among us gave voice to our common thought by saying, "I have the strange feeling that I have seen them all before." The silence having been broken, we all began laughing, relieved to be rid of our self-revealing reverie.

After another round of warm baked apples, our friends gradually left, taking with them armloads of the colorful homegrown Indian corn and gourds that had graced the festivities. The larger pumpkins still burned, and these were taken, too, as lanterns to light the way down the long, dark drive. As the candles grew dim in the distance, we were left again with the solitude of the canyon and the mingled aromas of cinnamon, clove, warm wine, and burning pumpkin flesh. It had been a grand celebration.

The next morning I rose early to clean up the debris. Those squash that had not joined the departing revelers remained in their places, covered with dew. The life had gone out of them. Their faces, wilted and blackened from fire, seemed frozen now and rigid. I gathered them all in the wheelbarrow and dumped them with the seeds and carvings on top of the compost pile, then returned to the rest of my work.

Life on the farm returned to normal, and except for occasional reminiscing, the Pumpkin Celebration faded into the rich but quiet backlog of experience. Then one day, while walking through the garden, I was seized by a spectacle so remarkable that I could hardly believe what I saw. I ran to the house to get Maggie and Pippin.

"The pumpkins!" I shouted. "They're alive again!"

We hurried back to the garden. Sure enough, these were not the same faces we had laid to rest on top of the compost. As we drew near, swarms of fruit flies rose into the autumn air. Molds were spreading over the squash in patches of white, grey, and black, and their features had begun to wrinkle and sag. The pumpkins were indeed alive, and they were growing old!

During the following days we watched the squash people age. Congressmen and actors, generals, workers, and poets, one and all, the same fate befell them. Some grew mellow, some fierce; some kept their wrinkled smiles to the very end, and some lost hope. And then one day, just as the last glimmer of life seemed to be ebbing from them, a beautiful thing happened. From the eye of a happy and contented old sage, a pumpkin seed sprouted and spread its leaves toward the sun. It would die soon in the frost, but nevertheless this was the final rite of renewal.

The Pumpkin Celebration had bitten us deeply. Pippin was only eighteen months old then, but when the next autumn rolled around he remembered the great event enough to be eager for the harvest. While I used the wheelbarrow, he used his little wagon, and together we brought the squash in.

The day of the festivities broke clear and cold. We arranged decorations of chrysanthemums, Indian corn, gourds, and autumn leaves. On an old crate in their midst we placed a special reminder of our heritage and the common heritage of all men —six skeletons of the squash people whose shells were hard enough to resist the process of decay. They had survived the compost pile, and they were with us again, now as ancestors.

This time all our friends arrived with contributions for the feast, and what a feast it was. Every conceivable kind of dish appeared upon the scene. Each was a personal creation, and they all blended perfectly in an uncanny display of compatibility.

We carved our pumpkins as before, but we did not place them together on the tables. Instead, from a pile of old boards we constructed rafts, and after the sun set we took them, the candles, and all the squash people down to the shore of Bolinas Lagoon. High tide was just beginning to ebb; the lagoon was smooth, the air cold and still. The western sky turned slowly from turquoise to purple, and just above the horizon the new moon and its attendant planet hung as though suspended right over the water before us.

Everyone moved in silhouette now, and as our black forms merged and separated in a ghostly pattern against the darkening sky, once again the owl hooted from a nearby tree. We lit the pumpkins and placed them, singly or in groups, on the rafts. One by one the little boats were launched into the main channel, and slowly they drifted out and away across the water. Once again we were silent. It was as though we had bid farewell to our good friends and wished them well on an unknown and perilous journey. For a while we could see their faces, and they were a mixed and motley crew; but soon they were only thirty-five little spots of light and thirty-five reflections in the dark water. At last they were gone. But not everyone gave up the vigil. Half a dozen people had brought their binoculars, and these were passed among us until the count had dwindled away to nothing and we were numb with cold. Full-grown people looking at pumpkins with binoculars in the dead of night! It was another incredible celebration.

We walked back into the canyon with a few remaining jack-o-lanterns to light the way. Over a final round of hot coffee, we discussed the fate of the voyagers. Whatever the consideration, we assumed that we would never see them again.

We were wrong. The next day clouds moved in from the Pacific, and that night the first big storm of winter lashed the coast. Strong winds wailed through the canyon, and white caps broke against the shore of the lagoon. When the clouds finally lifted, Maggie, Pippin, and I walked down to the edge of the water to see what damage might have been done, and there they were, a dozen pumpkin faces looking up at us from beneath the rippling water! We hunted for more and found nearly all of them, strewn along the shore for two miles in either direction. The voyagers had come home again.

What few we could carry we took back to the garden and placed on the compost pile to return to the soil that had given them life.

Counting the Joys

Our search for a more independent and satisfying way of life has just begun. In some areas we have made rewarding gains; in others we have come just far enough along the path of self-discovery to realize that the search will never end, for we ourselves are gradually changed by the journey itself.

Before new life can reach for the sun, its roots must first be planted deeply in the earth. There was a time not so long ago, before this age of rapid change, when the roots of our culture were embedded in the continuity of tradition, family, and community. This heritage we have tried to find again by returning to the basic laws of nature and to the strength of our own history.

We have been drawn to our family heritage and to the history of the land upon which we live. Though most of the old-timers are gone, and with them the knowledge, the spirit, and the shortcomings that could have taught us much of what we need to know, we have nevertheless tried to save what remains, for the knowledge of the past is our only bank account against the future.

The history of the herons and egrets that nest each year at Audubon Canyon Ranch, and of the lagoon that supports them and a host of other species, is a microcosm of man's effects upon the land throughout the entire history of his presence. This is a history that contains lessons for us all.

The giant redwoods among which the Miwoks once camped and
hunted were felled for the building of San Francisco; the
lagoon filled with silt from erosion of the naked watershed.
Mountain lions, bears, and the sacred coyotes were exterminated.
They have not returned, but the redwoods and other trees have
grown again. Now this place is a sanctuary, and the land has
begun to heal.

The Indian encampments are gone and with them an entire tribe and culture. The healing came too late for them. In their place the old house and farm were built. In a century they, too, have changed as various residents have come and gone, for only people can mend houses and give them life, just as people alone can mend their communities, their culture, and their way of life.

Near the house there is an ancient, gnarled buckeye where
Pippin often plays, cradled by the strength and
immensity of its limbs. Here at last perhaps new life and
old will merge toward a stronger future.

The old buckeye survived mostly because
it wasn't needed for firewood and it
wasn't good for lumber. These reasons
are not enough. Who will there be a
hundred years from now, or even
tomorrow, to protect the intricate, life-
sustaining natural systems from our
own lack of perception? Perhaps only
those who love and understand this world.

139

The very survival of life on this planet may depend upon recognizing
the need to blend mind and spirit, and the simple need we have for
each other. These age-old callings, too long denied in our culture, finally
welled up within us as a rite of renewal, the autumn pumpkin celebration.

Each year our friends gather for the carving of the squash harvest. It is a time not for the intellect but for the spirit. We visit and feast, and when it is dark, all the assembled squash people are given life by fire, a great procession of faces staring back at us as mirror images of our inner selves.

Sometimes we launch the pumpkins upon the quiet water of the lagoon and watch, transfixed and silent, as the little boats and their passengers drift toward the sea. Perhaps this act is only a symbol of the larger voyage each of us seems to yearn for.

We have begun to understand that the entire harvest celebration is only a symbol, for all of life, even with its tribulations, is a celebration. It is a great cycle of birth, death, and survival to be shared in the very act of living. Life itself is the greatest of all rites of renewal. The intellect may acknowledge this, but the spiritual side of man knows it from longer experience. Blending anew the intellect and the spirit may give man the strength and wisdom to live at peace with himself and in balance with the world. The way of life we have embarked upon is slowly giving us the strength to begin this inner journey.

6

ALMOST HOME

Many experiences must feed an idea, and many ideas are required to feed a philosophy of life. Our three-year beginning at Audubon Canyon Ranch has been a rich collection of experiences. They have given rise to a continuing process of soul-searching and evaluation between us as well as with our family, our friends, and our students. From this sharing, a rudimentary life philosophy has begun to emerge.

There is only one big hill that we must climb in a lifetime. We are born at the bottom of it, and we die however far toward its summit we have climbed by the end of our days. This hill has been known among all peoples since the dawn of man as "Know Thyself."

Some believe that to reach the top of this hill is the ultimate goal of man. Some hold that it is to a place higher than the summit that man must aspire. We believe that the view from the bottom is as grand as that from the highest rock; that the journey itself—every pebble, every drop of water, every plant, every animal, and every person encountered along the way—is the most important part of being human; and that any exploration that may exist beyond this journey is another adventure to be pursued in its own time.

Man is of dual nature; he is part intellectual and pragmatic, part emotional and spiritual. We hold the basic premise that the growth of the conscious mind and the growth of the psyche are as two feet searching for the same path. Only by recognizing both and learning to appreciate the wisdom that each contains do we stand a chance of becoming whole, and only with two feet working in harmony can the hill be climbed with time and energy to spare for vision.

This is a lonely journey of a lifetime. Maggie and I walk together when we can, share the excitement, the joy, and the disappointment we encounter as we explore, and support each other when we need to rest or even retreat. But each of us knows also that our paths must sometimes be separate and that in the darkest moments we must be alone on the hill of self-discovery.

A sense of these ideas has been with us for a long time; the notions themselves have grown toward expression gradually through experience, and they remain always open for review. It is upon them above all, however, that we shape our lives.

During these three years we have searched for an ecologically sound and satisfying way of life that places us close to the natural world we cherish. In taking stock of our progress, we realize that this has been equally a search for family, community, and, in the largest sense, that elusive place called home. By the very nature of this journey, we have gained a deeper understanding of ourselves and the values which have slowly evolved within us.

A wise friend who had seen much of life once told me that there are two things that make life worth living. One is meaningful companionship, and the other is meaningful function. Maggie and I found each other because we had begun to know ourselves just enough to recognize the kind of companionship that fulfilled our needs. By choosing a way of life in which our patterns of growth are more in harmony than in conflict, this companionship has been vastly strengthened, and our lives are richer as a result.

We have found meaningful function by following our deepest interests and standing always by our most firmly held convictions. Yet neither sustaining our companionship nor refining our function has been automatic. Both have required constant vigilance and frequent hard work. This process of refinement acts like natural selection itself, for we believe that only by carefully eliminating ideas and traits of behavior that do not seem to work for us and by rigorously screening the options that present themselves to us will our actions, our attitudes, and our spirits evolve.

In the process of earning a living, we have gradually become more selective in our choice of work. As time has passed, this choice has more often been made in keeping with patterns of personal growth, but for many years we have been guided as well by two other paramount considerations. The first is this: what effect does our work have upon the human, physical, and biological resources of the world?

Columnist Herb Caen of the *San Francisco Chronicle* once observed that "people who talk about the quality of life, as an avocation, and destroy it as a vocation are people badly in need of an examination of conscience." Conversely, we have been equally aware that many people who work for a better world on the job continue to strive for extravagant consumption and materialistic forms of leisure as a way of life. What began for us as a means of job selection has therefore become a search for an entire process of living that will tread more gently upon the world.

The second consideration is this: how good a job can we do? Very early in our lives Maggie and I realized that we did the best work when we were doing what we loved and enjoyed most. By rejecting work that did not parallel our interests and our gifts, we have not found it difficult to do a good job. Over the years we have tackled many assignments, and we have never been satisfied with performing below our best capabilities. We have discovered that hard work and thoroughness are attributes more scarce in our culture today than they once were.

By challenging our abilities, improving our self-discipline, and seeing each job through as long as we felt we could be effective, we have helped our capabilities to grow and with them our sense of satisfaction. For many years jobs have come to us instead of the reverse. As the number of options has increased, so also has our freedom of choice.

Primitive peoples lived by the simplest form of economy. With a minimum division of labor, they traded their time directly for shelter, sustenance, and spiritual fulfillment. Since the invention of barter, and especially since the rise of currency as a means of exchange, the individual has faced with increasing uncertainty these questions: For what should I trade my time? Must time be exchanged for money alone or for experience also? How much time should be given in pursuit of external commodities and how much in pursuit of internal growth?

Technology and a proliferated division of labor have long been touted, particularly since the industrial revolution, as a means of achieving leisure time. For all but the wealthy, this notion has largely proven to be a myth, for as one reaches ever farther for a higher standard of living and increased security, the striving itself becomes the greatest consumer of time and energy. The average citizen of the industrialized nations has less free time for leisure, community interaction, creative expression, and spiritual growth than did the hunting-and-gathering peoples of old.

In moving again toward a simpler way of life, we have found that time is the most precious of all commodities. It is made all the more precious because history cannot be reversed. There is no way to escape the fact that time must now be exchanged for more than basic survival. Even if one were to reduce his standard of living to the level enjoyed by the ancient food gatherer, he would at the very least have to reckon with the matter of land. There is a price on living space now in all but the wildest corners of the world, and whether it takes the direct form of time or the indirect form of money, that price must be paid.

Because of this alone, it is harder to lead a simple life than it once was. On top of this must be added whatever standard of living one is willing to settle for and whatever responsibilities one is willing to assume toward the family and the community at large. Try as one might to avoid it, some money must sooner or later exchange hands, for money has become as important to us as language.

For the most part, it is true that goods and services cost more today if purchased by time than by money. A few hours' work for wages will buy more vegetables in the supermarket than a week's work can grow in the garden. This peculiar twist of economics is a relatively new phenomenon, one that has been made possible at a high price, the final effects of which cannot yet be firmly evaluated. That hidden cost is consumption of energy —the vast quantities of energy that run the agricultural and industrial system from which modern commercial goods and services emanate.

The more we have attempted to do things for ourselves, the more conscious we have become of time. There is a point beyond which one simply does not have time enough both to provide his own goods and services, and to earn money. To find a way to balance one against the other is the greatest challenge of the simple life today.

We have learned from our short experience that nothing gained in life is without its price. Civilized man has achieved better health, longer life, and increased comfort by sacrificing a simple economy, closeness to the natural world, and, to a great extent, fulfillment of the spirit. By rejecting in turn some of these achievements, Maggie and I have lost a few of the comforts of modern civilization and a bit of what others might call security. But we have also learned that costs and gains can be measured by many yardsticks, for of the benefits we have reaped by returning to the land and the rhythms of nature, by doing for ourselves with our own labor and ingenuity, and by including each other and our son in work as well as play, none can be defined in the language of present-day economics. These benefits belong to a more ancient economy, and the joy we have experienced in finding them also lies beyond the realm of contemporary calculation.

Many people, even some who know us well, have suggested that though our ideals are commendable, they are not necessarily practical in modern America. It is true that by living in the country, we are able to pursue a life-style that is to some extent beyond the reach of most Americans. Yet on the other hand, few of the changes we have made in our own way of life could not be adapted on a smaller scale by nearly every urban family.

Think for a moment of all the suburban gardens you have seen, many of them located upon the richest agricultural soil in the world. What plants can you remember seeing there? Junipers and a hundred other nonproductive exotics like them, with perhaps a fruit tree here and there whose produce goes begging. And lawns! There must be hundreds of thousands of acres of lawn in the United States, and as many gas-eating machines to tend them. In China one seldom if ever sees a lawn; every square foot of arable soil in the areas where people live is put to productive use. We once had a tiny yard in town, but in that precious space we grew nearly all of our vegetables and some of our fruit, and we did it in the only time available to most Americans—evenings and weekends. Neighborhood children and adults alike stopped to enjoy the beauty of sunflowers and the lushness of our productive greenery.

Think of all the lights burning in unoccupied rooms, and all the neon signs and office lights blazing all night long so that nearly a generation of urban American children have never seen a star-filled sky. Think of the millions of thermostats set at 70° when 65° would be just as comfortable, and of the untold millions of superfluous electric gadgets that inflate the gross national product. Who needs an electric toothbrush or an electric carving knife?

Go to the nearest city dump some day and see for yourself the tons of garbage buried each day in the ground. Where has all this substance of the earth come from, and where will it go? Have you ever put styrofoam in a compost pile? Have you ever burned a plastic food wrapper and smelled the toxic fumes?

Our basic standard of living does not pose the gravest problem, even though our disproportionate use of the world's resources is partly the result of it. No, it is more the unique phenomenon of conspicuous consumption that lies at the heart of diminishing resources and a plundered planet, and the reduction of this factor lies easily within the grasp of every consumer. The sooner every American understands that an electric carving knife is directly connected to a drowned river valley, a strip-mined mountain range, or a poisonous tank of atomic waste, the more quickly we can return to a rational state of balance with our fragile world.

For better or worse, there has always been an elite in every civilization. This perhaps the world could afford, but the world cannot afford an entire elite nation—actually a whole elite culture of people in many nations who have more than their share.

Nor has a life-style of conspicuous consumption brought us mental or psychic reward. Show me a king who is happier than a peasant. And we are all kings when we live extravagantly at the expense of other men and of creatures beyond our own kind.

If reducing consumption lies within reach of most urban Americans, the changes that have come about in our attitudes are even more attainable. Though our days are full on the farm, we have slowed our pace of daily living and certainly the pace of striving. So also have we lowered our need for comfort just as surely as we have reduced our hunger for sweets—by doing so one small step at a time. We have come to believe that when individuals, like species, lack challenge, they become weak; so we deliberately keep physical as well as mental challenges before us, that we may rise to their demands and grow accordingly. Our appreciation of all living things, our understanding of other people, our love for each other, and our commitment to self-exploration have all grown deeper in these three years.

These changes have been stimulated by our changing way of life, but more than that, we have wanted them and actively sought them. Not a one is dependent upon country living. The time and the effort we have spent are similarly available to anyone who has decided that these attitudes are worth searching for.

The most rewarding change of all, however, has been our increasing awareness of children. Glen Doman, director of the Institute for the Achievement of Human Potential, has observed, "It is surprising that the majority of us have lost the constant and intimate relationship with our children that is so important to the child's entire future and which can be so splendidly pleasurable to us. The pressures of our society and of our culture have robbed us of this so quietly that we have been unaware of the fact that it is gone, or perhaps we have been unaware that it ever existed."

Children are the future of our society. They are equally the future of our species. Most important, however, Maggie and I have discovered that children are the finest of all teachers. Learning this is available to us all.

We began our journey because we were dissatisfied. We are still not satisfied. As we think about where we have been and where we are going, we recognize more than ever that the home we are looking for is much more than a beautiful house in the country. Home is a place, a family, a culture, a heritage, and a way of life all wrapped into one.

Living close to the land, living anywhere for that matter, was never meant to be a solitary process. Even though we have achieved a certain level of companionship, we realize that there are many levels of family and community sharing that remain for us to find.

Extended families are not easily restored. We have come to value our independence and our privacy just as our parents have. Many of the common needs that otherwise would draw us together are still too easily denied or fulfilled in other ways. Our communities, like the boomtowns of early days, are still largely fragmented aggregations of people assembled more by circumstance than by real human needs. We still live in a culture that for the most part does not support the values we hold in trust.

Even our heritage has been partly lost. Our culture lives in the present, for it tends to be blind to the past and negligent of the future. Instead of adding the new to the old, we throw the old away and move on to something not yet proven. Thus in a generation or two we lose whole banks of knowledge and a great deal of attendant wisdom. The tragedy of this is that wisdom cannot always be assessed in the present. We don't know what part of it we may eventually need. It is our only bank account against the future.

In our own small corner of life we have felt this loss. Ironically the very city that my father and uncle abandoned for the country as children dammed the Mokelumne River to feed the city water supply and thus buried forever the family farm to which they fled and from which they learned their love for the natural world. Every wild hill and marsh I explored as a child is now a road, a subdivision, or an asphalt school yard—and I am only thirty years old. The creek in which I learned almost everything I know about the natural order of streams and aquatic life is now a concrete channel. No child in that valley will ever again have the opportunity I had. What is worse, no child in that valley will ever truly know what he has missed.

At Audubon Canyon Ranch we have helped to stem this tide of adverse change. The Ranch is a microcosm of American history. The Miwok Indians, who lived the original simple life, quickly vanished before the onslaught of the white man. The early settlers ran roughshod over the land. They stripped the hills of timber, and the lagoon filled with silt; it will remain shallow. They

hunted almost everything that moved, until the mountain lions, coyotes, and bears were eliminated; they have not returned.

Eventually these canyons became dairy ranches, and the bluffs of coastal scrub became patches of invasive weeds. As the dairy business waned, the ranch houses were occupied by gentlemen farmers who no longer took their sustenance from the land. Gradually the hills recovered, trees grew again upon them, and herons and egrets began nesting in the canyon redwoods; but the human heritage, the spirit that once filled the old houses even in the plundering pioneer days, had somehow dwindled.

By the time Audubon Canyon Ranch acquired the canyon in which we now live, much of its history was gone. The big cow barn had been torn down, and most of the orchard had been destroyed. The wooden walls and ceilings of the ranch house had been covered with plasterboard, its frame windows changed to plate glass, its wood stoves replaced with an electric range and heaters. The house had been made modern even while it stood among echoes of a former farm.

On moving day we tore up the wall-to-wall carpets, sanded the paint from the oak floors, and moved in our old family furniture. We threw open the doors, unsealed the windows, and let the fresh coastal air flow once more through the rooms. Bit by bit the house began to live again. Spiders moved in between the bricks of the fireplace, bees and bats moved into the attic, and a lizard took up residence behind the woodbin. We installed a cookstove, built bookshelves and worktables, and constructed a dining table from virgin redwood planks, still full of square nails, from the longhouse.

Audubon Canyon Ranch is a sanctuary now, set aside in perpetuity for nature education and the preservation of wildlife. Nature heals in time most of the wounds inflicted by man. Through the wisdom of many people this healing process has been allowed to happen at the Ranch. But people alone can heal the wounds inflicted upon houses and the history and way of life houses reflect. Our small role in this regard has been a rich and pleasurable experience, but it will never fully compensate for the things from our childhood that have been lost. We and our children and our grandchildren will be able to return to Audubon Canyon Ranch, but I can never return to the creek of my childhood.

I was sitting at my desk writing one autumn evening when a stonefly from the stream flew in through the window and circled around the light. The last of the herons and egrets had settled for the night to roost in the trees across the canyon. They would soon be leaving for the winter, but we would see them again in the spring as others would after us for a hundred other springs and more. How strange, I thought, is this sense of history that besets our species.

I could snuff this little creature out, I thought, with a mere rub of my thumb. I could kill the egrets for a few hat plumes as others had done before me. But why? Who am I to say what lives or what dies, beyond what my family needs for sustenance? The birds squawking in the trees through the half-light of evening have been around far longer than I or my kind, and this stonefly is older still. Its ancestors were among the first winged creatures to test the wind. Egrets and stoneflies just as surely as wood stoves and old houses are part of Pippin's heritage; he knows them and will remember them, just as I remember them from my own childhood.

Even more, these creatures are part of the web of life in which everything alive is involved. I remembered the moment of Pippin's birth and the sense of heritage with which it had filled me. The same wisdom that cares for the heritage of man, I realized, must also care for the heritage of all other living things.

This Maggie and I believe. We have come this far at least on our journey of a lifetime.

Western man has gone through a long period of outward pioneering and expansion. Through our science and technology we have explored the world, even conquered it. We have come to know the world as we know our own face in the mirror, in nearly every aspect save one: what lies behind that mirrored image. We look at ourselves, and because our lips do not move, we assume we do not speak. We have nearly lost the ancient ability to hear our inner selves. With our instruments we know the heartbeat of the sun that gives us light, and we listen to the pulsing of distant stars. But the searching, groping, sometimes screaming inner voice of man goes unnoticed in the bewildering firestorm of contemporary life.

There is a level of thinking and speaking in man that involves primordial images. These images are the symbols that form the language of our dreams. They speak always within us even though we may not hear them. The farther we have removed ourselves by our culture from the conditions under which we evolved, the greater have been our difficulties, because in the process we have hidden both the food and the voice of the psyche.

Maggie and I have begun to see that we are not simple human beings. Within the deepest recesses of our nature we are discovering our innate complexities. The original simple life lies forever beyond our grasp, for we are children of the twentieth century. Science has touched and blended with the spirit. No religion could now sustain this spirit; no dogma or simple tradition alone could hold us. We strive to know what is not yet known. We stand always at the edge of a void, and the spaces before us grow larger the farther we penetrate them.

In our inner lives there will never be simplicity. We can only hope to live simply without so that we might be less encumbered on our larger journey within. This above all is the heritage we wish to give to our son and to all children. Out of these primitive strivings may yet emerge man.

About This Book

The Words

In both the living and the retelling, *Almost Home* has evolved as a thoroughly mutual endeavor. The whole affair began as a life experience and only later developed the focus that enabled it to fall together in time, piece by piece, between two covers.

Once the living itself had assumed some natural structure, we developed a chapter file of manila folders that reflected this organization and began a tentative sorting of selected photographs that were emerging from our experiences. The writing began as, and until the very last remained, an endless series of paper scraps—the backs of receipts, discarded mail, envelopes, pieces of brown bags—upon which we jotted discoveries, ideas, feelings, and quotations as they crystallized from explorations, readings, solitary ruminations, or long discussions around the dinner table or in bed late at night. To survive our rare forays into town, we began to use automobile trips as a prime time for this honing of our thoughts, to the degree that we often overshot our destination by many miles and were frequently late for appointments. The resulting shreds of paper were gathered now and then from dashboard, coat pockets, and various corners of the house, dropped into the appropriate chapter files, and for the time being forgotten.

As the inevitable time of fruition advanced upon us, I took the scraps of paper from the chapter one file, read and sorted them, and taped them to a huge board in the order they assumed in my mind. This board remained before me until the writing of the chapter was completed.

It was an exciting process, a new kind of discovery in itself. Here on the board was a treasure of morsels, some written by Maggie, some by me, and some gleaned from the writing or conversation of others. Many were deeply thought-provoking, some were hilarious, and others seemed not to belong at all; most were nearly illegible, particularly those scribbled in the middle of the night or in the moving car. Nevertheless, I began and, over a period of weeks, wrote on the backs of old letters until all the chapters were done. For every hour I spent at my desk at least three were spent under the influence of that marvelous procrastination which only a vegetable garden can engender.

I wrote down everything that either seemed relevant at the time or needed to be purged from my system, until the manuscript fairly bulged at the seams. It is a good thing that behind every writer stands an editor. I read each day's work aloud to Maggie, whose influence upon the ideas and their final expression has been of immeasurable significance. Though I put the words on paper, the book was written by both of us, for Maggie functioned as author as well as editor. Thus the first draft was forged.

After patient deciphering and typing by Claire Philpott (who,

being married to a printer, should have known better than to accept such a task) and further cutting, reshuffling, and splicing, the manuscript went to editor Pat Kollings at American West. Pat and Maggie, in their quiet way, share an uncanny intuition regarding both my nature and the English language. With talent and tenderness, Pat performed the final surgery. Most of the soapbox speeches and much extraneous material needed to be condensed or removed. After one quick rewrite the manuscript was done, and I left for a month in the Galápagos Islands while Maggie began her engravings.

The Illustrations

The wood engravings that open the chapters and all the linocuts that accompany the text were done by Maggie. The original sketches were rendered in some cases from photographs we took around the Ranch and in others directly from life. Wood for the larger cuts was carefully selected from virgin redwood planks removed during a minor alteration of the 120-year-old longhouse; the linocuts were made on ship deck linoleum. The actual carving was done with a set of Sanders wood engraving tools. Using a small Vandercook proof press, the final prints were made on rice paper and reduced 45% for reproduction in the book.

Though Maggie has been developing an artistic form of expression in various media for several years, she had carved only a handful of blocks prior to beginning the work for this book. Our printer friend, Arlen Philpott, who helped Maggie assemble her cutting and printing equipment and was the first to use her work, and Dannelle Pfeiffer, designer at American West who saw the prints carefully through their final reproduction, both offered valuable support and advice; but for the most part Maggie is learning to cut and print on her own through experimentation.

The idea of incorporating engravings arose rather late in the evolution of the book, and so they were done toward the very last. It took her just three months to settle upon and refine the technique and complete all twenty-seven prints. Though I waded through drifts of wood and linoleum chips for the duration, shared the cooking and some of the house chores, and fought to keep one square foot of my desk open for the typewriter while Maggie covered the remaining three tables in our workroom as well, it was indeed a pleasure to watch her joyously discovering a new skill and to share my suggestions as she had so freely shared hers during the writing.

Unlike the engravings, the photography was begun as soon as we moved to the Ranch, before the book had even jelled, and continued throughout the project. In some ways the photographs formed the backbone from which the rest of the skeleton of the book was hung. Though I have been working as a photographer for ten years, Maggie took her first pictures during the creation of our last book, *This Living Earth*, and six of her photographs appear in this book.

Maggie does not photograph often, but when she does it is usually because she has seen something that inspires her. Sometimes I do the same, running with camera in hand after an ephemeral scene or happening, but more often I wait until I am in the mood for photography and then spend a few hours prowling around in search of subjects that catch my eye.

We both use work-worn 35mm Nikkormat cameras with built-in meters, and three basic lenses, which we share. Though we have developed a love for tools in general as we have learned to do more with our own hands, the automobile and the camera are two tools for which we have only the most detached interest. We use small-format equipment, in the most minimum amounts, because it is the simplest quality equipment available, requires the least amount of fuss, and places the smallest impediment between us and the actual experiences that draw us to the natural world in the first place. Though photography is an intensely satisfying form of expression, one that helps to focus our experience and our vision, it is still the seeing itself that quickens our pulse and offers us the deepest rewards.

This book represents a photographic departure for me in two important respects. Until this project I had beeen almost exclusively an interpreter of the natural world. Perhaps because of this specific focus, perhaps also out of a reluctance to impose upon others, I have not been drawn to photographing people. The publisher of this book, George Pfeiffer, may have altered that stance permanently when he suggested, even before Pippin was born, that I make a photographic record of the growth of our child. Though it was no doubt easiest to begin this change with an infant as subject, nevertheless much discipline was required to begin to see people as photographic material, especially members of my own family, whose moods and activities I had taken for granted. In spite of this, the result has been an inspiring peek through a door I had somehow never before dared to enter.

The second change that has recently overtaken me is the use of a tripod, that infernal contraption, peculiar to surveyors and photographers, that anchors its user firmly to the ground like a tree and deprives him of his inherent animal mobility. Were it not for my intense dislike of the tripod, I probably would be using a large-format camera and would have missed forever the chance to explore as a photographer the minutiae of the grass-roots world that have given me such pleasure and so many wet bellies.

Nonetheless, the more I have studied the results, particularly as they have been reproduced on the printed page, the more aware I have become of the need for sharpness. Not all pictures and not all areas of a given picture demand sharpness, however, and my selective adventures with a tripod have therefore been restricted to those subjects the eye wants to see sharply, those times when mobility is not crucial, and those instances when only sheer laziness would otherwise prevent its use.

Recording the image is only the first part of good photography. Just as in writing, it is the editing that provides the essential polishing of one's work. This was put most succinctly by photographer Steve Crouch who, when asked the difference between an amateur and a professional photographer, replied, "The size of his wastebasket." I do all my own technical editing, but the selection of pictures and their final arrangement in the book were done by Maggie and me together.

The Whole

Making a book, particularly one with photographs, is a long and complex process involving numerous compromises that begin almost with the conception of the idea. The creation of the basic material, though it may take the most time, is really only the beginning. Once a book goes into production and eventually to market, it must face all the technical, economic, and aesthetic realities of the publishing industry, and finally the reaction of an audience. For the creator, who stands to have his inner self exposed, this often seems a strident and perilous journey. Tremendous amounts of energy and resources—the very same we urge all to conserve are consumed by the technology necessary to produce a book; accepting this has for us been the most difficult compromise of all.

Books are made by publishers and printers, as well as by authors. In these last steps numerous people provide the talent and craftsmanship that hone a book toward its final quality. As in all of life, there are periodic difficulties, even crises, but this book has been an unusually happy experience for all of us who have worked together on it.

One night very late we were returning, exhausted and rather bruised, from a hectic day fighting traffic in the Big City. As we approached the Ranch, our dog, Bo, stood up knowingly with nose alert, his feet on the back of the seat. "Yes, Bo, we're almost home," I said. Pippin stirred in Maggie's lap, awoke, and cried a little. I began singing a little round to him, "We're almost home, Pippin; we're almost home." That night another scrap of paper went into the file, marked "possible title."

This has been a three-year beginning. Pippin is growing, and we also are changing. A book is a small chapter in one's life, a seed nurtured at first, then thrown to the elements that it might grow its own fruit. Meanwhile the search we have begun continues along a path the destination of which may forever remain unknown, for this is the destiny of man.

Photographic Details

Pippin watching the sunset from a grassy ridge above Bolinas Lagoon. Micro-Nikkor 55mm; Kodachrome X. PAGES 2-3

Great egret, *Casmerodius albus*, flying over Bolinas Lagoon at sunset, returning to the rookery to feed its young. Vivitar 500mm, hand held; High Speed Ektachrome. PAGE 4

The old ranch house at Audubon Canyon Ranch, built in the 1870s; looking toward the lagoon from beneath a great California live oak. Micro-Nikkor 55mm on a tripod; Kodachrome II. PAGE 7

Calypso orchid, *Calypso bulbosa*, blooming in the spring beneath a Douglas fir on the ridge of Mount Tamalpais above the Ranch. A bit of lens flare was used intentionally to simulate sunbeams streaming through the trees. Micro-Nikkor 55mm; Kodachrome II. PAGE 8

Pippin at a few months of age asleep in the garden, photographed by Maggie. Micro-Nikkor 55mm; Kodachrome X. PAGE 9

Early morning fog of summer covering San Francisco Bay, taken from the ridge of Mount Tamalpais with Mount Diablo in the distance. On errand day we often leave at dawn to enjoy the view from the winding mountain road leading toward the city. Micro-Nikkor 55mm, with the camera resting on a roadside post for a long exposure; Kodachrome II. PAGE 10

The web of a long-jawed spider in the marsh, covered with condensation. Micro-Nikkor 55mm; High Speed Ektachrome. PAGE 11

A waterfall beneath the redwoods in the canyon, when the leaves of elk's clover, *Aralia californica*, have turned golden in late fall. Bushnell 28mm on a tripod for an exposure of one second, more or less; Kodachrome II. PAGE 12

Fallen leaves of California bay laurel, *Umbellularia californica*, on a rainy day in autumn. Micro-Nikkor 55mm; Kodachrome X. PAGE 13

Storm clouds advancing over Bolinas Lagoon in winter, looking south toward San Francisco. Canyons and ridges to the left are part of the Ranch. Bushnell 28mm; Kodachrome II. PAGES 14-15

A young raccoon photographed by Maggie in a ranch yard pear tree. Micro-Nikkor 55mm; Kodachrome X. PAGE 33

Maggie and Pippin making a discovery among a field of California poppies, *Eschscholtzia californica*. Nikkor 105mm; Kodachrome II. PAGE 34

Their find in the poppies, a recently emerged California sister, *Heterochroa californica*. Micro-Nikkor 55mm; Kodachrome II. PAGE 35

Pippin blowing cattail fuzz in the marsh on a winter day. Nikkor 105mm; Kodachrome II. PAGE 36

Cattail seed plumes caught on rushes, photographed straight into the sun. Taking a reading under these conditions is purely a guess, but I usually read the meter off to the side a bit and work from there. Micro-Nikkor 55mm; Kodachrome II. PAGE 37

Pippin helping the vines to climb the poles of his large, walk-in bean tepee, taken by Maggie with the Nikkor 105mm; Kodachrome X. PAGE 38, LEFT

All of us working in the summer garden, harvesting potatoes behind the lettuce patch. Our friend Tom Nordstrom helped us take this shot. Bushnell 28mm; Kodachrome II. PAGES 38-39

The leaf of a cauliflower, backlit in early morning. Micro-Nikkor 55mm; Kodachrome II. PAGE 40

Pippin inspecting a purple cauliflower before sunrise. Micro-Nikkor 55mm on a tripod; Kodachrome II. PAGE 41

Purple or "decorative" kale, a favorite item of barter and an excellent feast for the eye as well as the stomach, taken on an overcast day. Micro-Nikkor 55mm on a tripod; Kodachrome II. PAGE 42

Italian broccolini, a superb vegetable uncommon to this country; the seeds came from Rome. Micro-Nikkor 55mm on a tripod; Kodachrome II. PAGE 43, TOP

A slice through the middle of an orange, abducted for the photograph from a fruit bowl in which berry juice provided a bit of staining. Backlit; Micro-Nikkor 55mm; Kodachrome II. PAGE 43, BOTTOM

Maggie milking the matriarch of our herd, Sunflower, and sharing a little with a surprised Pippin. Micro-Nikkor 55mm; Kodachrome II. PAGE 44

Pippin being licked by a still-wet, newborn goat kid. Micro-Nikkor 55mm; Kodachrome II. PAGE 45

Some of Maggie's homespun yarn, dyed with plant colors as follows, from left to right: lavender from wild grape; red, madder root; brown, coffee; light pink, cochineal (a scale insect, not a plant); blue-grey, sunflower seeds; gold, turmeric; light yellow, California poppy flowers; dark pink, cochineal; tan, tea. Various mordants were used. Micro-Nikkor 55mm on a tripod; Kodachrome II. PAGE 46

Pippin in a cap spun from wool and the underfur of goat and dog (English sheepdog and husky); Maggie's spinning wheel from New Zealand. Micro-Nikkor 55mm; Kodachrome X. PAGE 47

A section of comb foundation from the beehives, only one side of which has been built upon. Looking from the unbuilt side with flat front light, one can see the bottom layer of pollen that had been added to each cell, each color representing a different flower source. Micro-Nikkor 55mm; Kodachrome II. PAGE 48

Craig Curley, Tom Nordstrom, and I prowling through the marsh; taken by Maggie with the Micro-Nikkor 55mm and Kodachrome II. PAGE 81

A newly emerged dragonfly, hardening its wings—an excellent subject for backlight. Micro-Nikkor 55mm; Kodachrome II. PAGE 82

Pacific giant salamander, *Dicamptodon ensatus*, from along streams in the redwood region, reaches a length of twelve inches. Micro-Nikkor 55mm; taken in the shade with High Speed Ektachrome. PAGE 83

A backlit caterpillar of the day-flying ctenuchid moth, *Ctenucha multifera*, photographed on its food plant, a rush in the marsh. Micro-Nikkor 55mm; Kodachrome II. PAGES 82-83

The "freeway" tracks of earthworms on mud, the morning after a flood in the canyon. Micro-Nikkor 55mm; Kodachrome X. PAGE 84

Wave ripples on the mud of the lagoon after a flood. Micro-Nikkor 55mm; High Speed Ektachrome. PAGE 85

Sixth-grade students exploring among cow parsnips. Nikkor 105mm; Kodachrome X. PAGE 86

Blossoms of the cow parsnip, *Heracleum lanatum*, seen from beneath. The young leaves of this plant are quite good eating. Nikkor 105mm; Kodachrome X. PAGE 87

A student learning to spin. Lens flare transmits the warm-light feeling of the late afternoon. Micro-Nikkor 55mm; Kodachrome II. PAGE 88

The hands of another student spinning, this time on an overcast day. Micro-Nikkor 55mm; Kodachrome II. PAGE 89, TOP

One of the students kneading bread dough. Micro-Nikkor 55mm; Kodachrome II. PAGE 89, BOTTOM

The undersides of orange chantrelles, *Cantharellus cibarius*, one of the favorite mushrooms both here and in Europe, and masked tricholomas, *Tricholoma personatum*, noted for their good flavor and rich violet color when young. (Caution: unless you are an expert at identifying them, eating mushrooms can be hazardous to your health.) Micro-Nikkor 55mm on a tripod in overcast light; Kodachrome II. PAGE 90

"Elephantine" bark on the old California live oak, *Quercus agrifolia*, beneath which we gather chantrelles. Nikkor 105mm on a tripod in overcast light; Kodachrome II. PAGE 91

Euchloë creusa, a native member of the family Pieridae, whose larvae like my Chinese cabbage. This one is newly emerged, still on its empty pupal case. Micro-Nikkor 55mm; Kodachrome II. PAGE 92

A leaf from my ravaged squash patch after a visit by migrant sparrows. Micro-Nikkor 55mm; Kodachrome II. PAGE 93

A one-to-one detail of the neck feathers of a male California quail, *Lophortyx californica*, enlarged here ten times actual size. This bird was trapped for color marking and then released, as part of a student study. Micro-Nikkor 55mm; Kodachrome II. PAGES 94-95

California tortoiseshell butterflies, *Vanessa californica*, drinking on a hot summer day. Micro-Nikkor 55mm; Kodachrome X. PAGE 96

Door of the 120-year-old longhouse, photographed by Maggie. Micro-Nikkor 55mm on a tripod; Kodachrome X. PAGE 129

An old family quilt, made in the late 1880s by someone else in my family named Maggie; it now graces our dining-room wall. Micro-Nikkor 55mm on a tripod; window light from nearby; Kodachrome II. PAGE 130

Another view of the longhouse, taken through the petunias on an overcast summer day. Nikkor 105mm; Kodachrome II. PAGE 131

Primary and secondary feathers on the wing of a great blue heron, *Ardea herodias*, found dead from natural causes beneath the rookery. Micro-Nikkor 55mm; Kodachrome II. PAGE 132

One of the spectacular winter sunsets over the tidal channels of Bolinas Lagoon. Nikkor 105mm, hand held; Kodachrome II. PAGE 133

Bark of a second-growth redwood, *Sequoia sempervirens*, covered with a blue-green lichen. Micro-Nikkor 55mm; time exposure on a tripod in deep shade; Kodachrome II. PAGE 134

The old ranch house as a winter storm departs at sunset, brooding over the canyon behind. These rare moments of rich light seldom last more than seconds, just before the sun sinks behind Bolinas Mesa. Micro-Nikkor 55mm; Kodachrome II. PAGE 135

The "Great Buckeye" in winter. One of the largest specimens of *Aesculus californica* in the state, this tree has not appreciably changed in size since photos were taken of it in 1906. Bushnell 28mm; Kodachrome II. PAGES 136-137

Pippin in the multiple trunks of the "Great Buckeye," photographed by Maggie with a Nikkor 105mm lens and Kodachrome X. PAGE 137

A nearly one-to-one photograph of the head of a sunflower, showing the many disk flowers that give the daisy family the name Compositae. Micro-Nikkor 55mm on a tripod in overcast light; Kodachrome II. PAGES 138-139

Part of the autumn squash harvest. Micro-Nikkor 55mm on a tripod in overcast light; Kodachrome II. PAGE 140

Jo-Jo Philpott carving a passenger for one of the pumpkin boats. Nikkor 105mm; Kodachrome II. PAGE 141

A few of the assembled squash people, stacked three tiers deep among the squash leaves. Micro-Nikkor 55mm on a tripod; High Speed Ektachrome exposed for a few seconds. PAGES 142-143

Maggie and Pippin launching pumpkins in the lagoon at dusk. Micro-Nikkor 55mm on a tripod; Kodachrome II at 1 second. PAGE 144

Index

AUDUBON CANYON RANCH is located on Shoreline Highway approximately three miles north of Stinson Beach, in Marin County, California. The best time to visit the Ranch is during nesting season, about March 1 through July 4. The public is welcome on Saturdays, Sundays, and holidays from 10 a.m. to 4 p.m.; school and other groups admitted by appointment Tuesdays through Fridays. The Ranch is closed Mondays. Direct inquiries to: Audubon Canyon Ranch, Route 1, Stinson Beach, California 94970; telephone (415) 383-1644.

Body type: Kennerley by Mackenzie & Harris, Inc., San Francisco, California.
Display type: Trump Semi-Bold Condensed by Continental Graphics, Los Angeles;
Hadriano Stone Cut by Mackenzie & Harris, Inc.
Printing and binding by Graphics Art Center, Portland.

Design by Dannelle Lazarus Pfeiffer